THE
MICROWAVE
KITCHEN

THE
MICROWAVE
KITCHEN

CREATIVE RECIPES FOR MICROWAVE
AND COMBINATION COOKING

CECILIA NORMAN

Macdonald Orbis

A *Macdonald Orbis* BOOK

First published in Great Britain in 1987
by Macdonald & Co (Publishers) Ltd
London & Sydney

A member of BPCC plc

British Library Cataloguing in Publication Data

Norman, Cecilia
  Microwave kitchen
  1. Microwave cookery
  I. Title
  641. 5'882   TX832

ISBN 0-356-14540-9

Editor Julie Dufour
Art Editor Clive Hayball
Production David Meads
Designer Ingrid Mason
Photographer Nick Carman
Stylist Penny Mishcon
Home Economist Caroline Ellwood
Illustrations Alison Wisenfeld

I would like to thank Penny Morris, my home economist, and Hélène Albinsson
for their help in testing and checking the recipes, and Rebecca Underwood from
St Albans College and Ginette Brown from the Polytechnic of North London, who
are both student home economists with exceptional flair. The book would never
have been completed so quickly and efficiently without the support and help of
my steadfast husband, Laurie, and Jenny Pouncett, who shouldered the
secretarial work.

Filmset by Text Filmsetters Ltd
Printed in Great Britain by
Purnell Book Production Limited
Member of the BPCC Group

Macdonald & Co (Publishers) Ltd
Greater London House
Hampstead Road
London NW1 7QX

CONTENTS

INTRODUCTION

I am really pleased that the microwave oven is now an accepted appliance. Its attributes are at least appreciated and fears and doubts over its ability and safety have been dispelled. In our modern and rapidly changing way of life, our equipment must be fast, efficient and easy to maintain. Cooking facilities are of vital importance if you are not to continually exist on a diet of raw food. Since food is essential to life, then it is worth trying to equip yourself with the best appliances for your way of life.

The microwave is the most recent culinary innovation of importance and has much to commend it. Although best known for its ability to defrost and reheat, it also provides an excellent method of cooking. Food cooked by microwave is delicious and nutritious but should not be compared to dishes cooked by conventional methods – the results are bound to be different. The microwave excels at vegetable cookery, basic sauces, fish, poultry, minced meat, scrambled, poached and even boiled eggs, steamed puddings, jams, pickles and stewed fruit. It can be used for boiling, poaching and stewing, roasting and baking – although the latter two processes do not produce the same results as in conventional cooking as the microwave creates no dry heat. This can be a great advantage, since food particles that stick fast on normal oven walls, particularly when roasting or baking in fat, can be removed from the microwave by a simple once-over wipe with a damp cloth.

Among its other commendable qualities, the microwave is a superior defrosting device, as thawing by microwave is both quick and gentle. Gone for ever is that interminable wait while thawing at room temperature. Reheating – the next stage after thawing – is accomplished without deterioration, which can so often occur when plates of food are reheated by steaming or in the conventional oven. Neither of these systems is very good – steaming can only be used for very moist foods; reheating in an oven can result in dried-up, overcooked meals.

The microwave can cope with very small as well as larger quantities – how wonderful it is to be able to heat a single mug of milk or coffee or boil just enough water for a cup of tea. There is no need to put on the kettle or even use a saucepan as everything can be heated in the drinking vessel.

A few more examples of its versatility are the speed and ease with which chocolate melts, gelatine dissolves, herbs can be dried, and even an open jar of shoe polish can be softened in seconds.

Microwaving is fast, taking about a quarter of conventional cooking times, so fuel bills are reduced as much less electricity is consumed. Washing-up is reduced as well and, if you are in the habit of using a dishwasher, valuable space need not be taken up in the machine by the saucepans. The microwave is also portable and requires only a three-pin plug and socket so that, if you do move house, you can ▶

Peach crumble (*see page 24*)

◄ cook by microwave alone until the remaining gas and electric appliances are properly fixed.

The microwave oven does, however, have its limitations – it does not brown and cannot crispen on the outside while maintaining softness underneath. For example, soufflés or Yorkshire puddings are quite impossible to cook in the microwave.

There are so many books now available, including many of my own, which concentrate entirely on microwave cooking. While most of these recipes are very good, they can only work within the constraints of the microwave's abilities. An infinitely greater selection of dishes could be prepared by making use of all the available cooking equipment; each appliance should be used for the jobs it does best. The major part of this book is, therefore, devoted to recipes that include both microwave and conventional methods, opening up the full spectrum of your kitchen's breadth and power of cooking. Some people, like myself, enjoy cooking and even find it therapeutic, while others have to cook out of necessity, and a large number exist on convenience foods, most of which only need defrosting and heating. The microwave is just as useful for all these groups of people – they are all cooks, all have their specific needs, and each will benefit from a well-equipped kitchen.

I have approached writing this book in what I feel to be a realistic way and am sure that it will prove much more useful than 'just another microwave recipe book'.

WHAT IS IN THE BOOK

This book has been divided into five chapters. Chapter 1 gives a brief introduction to the microwave and a resumé of the different types of microwave presently available. Chapter 2 is concerned with the use of combination ovens and contains a small collection of recipes to guide you through. Should you decide on a microwave-only model and possess an efficient electric, gas or Aga cooker, you will be able to adapt both these and also the collection of traditional recipes in Chapter 3, which are cooked by combining microwave and conventional methods.

In Chapter 4 you will find dinner party recipes using microwave only, and in Chapter 5 there are the lessons in using microwaves and the basic microwave techniques and processes. I have specifically put this chapter at the back of the book because there will be a large number of readers who have already mastered these processes, but the instructions will be easy for new microwave users to find and handy for quick reference.

HOW TO USE THE RECIPES

The following points will help you understand the recipes and carry them out successfully.

1. All spoons are level: 1 tablespoon = 15ml; 1 teaspoon = 5ml.

2. Flour is plain unless otherwise stated.

3. Eggs are size 3 unless otherwise stated.

4. The recipes are given in both Metric and Imperial measures and these must not be mixed within the recipe.

5. The recipes assume that vegetables, fish, poultry, meat, etc. have been rinsed and trimmed before cooking.

6. Best results will be obtained if the recommended type and size of container is used. A very large bowl holds 2.8 litres/ 5 pints, a large bowl 2 litres/3½ pints, a medium bowl 1.1 litres/2 pints, a small bowl 570ml/1 pint.

7. Cooking times are only approximate.

8. Only microwave-suitable dishes should be used in a microwave oven. Dishes may be covered with a lid, an undecorated plate, greaseproof paper or suitable cling film.

9. When using combination ovens, the recipes should be cooked on the Celcius setting with the microwave at Defrost. When the oven is being preheated, the microwave should not be switched on.

10. In combination ovens, use ovenproof or flameproof glass or ceramics unless the manufacturers recommend otherwise. Plates and cling film are not suitable coverings.

11. Symbols have been included in Chapter 3 to show which appliance should be used.

▲▲ = cooking by microwave oven.

◀ = cooking by conventional methods.

SOLID MEASURES

Metric	Imperial	Metric	Imperial	Metric	Imperial
10 g	¼ oz	200 g	7 oz	1.75 kg	4–4½ lb
15 g	½ oz	225 g	8 oz	2 kg	4½–4¾ lb
20 g	¾ oz	250 g	9 oz	2.25 kg	5–5¼ lb
25 g	1 oz	300 g	10 oz	2.5 kg	5½–5¾ lb
40 g	1½ oz	325 g	11 oz	2.75 kg	6 lb
50 g	2 oz	350 g	12 oz	3 kg	7 lb
65 g	2½ oz	375 g	13 oz	3.5 kg	8 lb
75 g	3 oz	400 g	14 oz	4 kg	9 lb
90 g	3½ oz	425 g	15 oz	4.5 kg	10 lb
100 g	4 oz	450 g	1 lb (16 oz)	5 kg	11 lb
120 g	4½ oz	550 g	1¼ lb	5.5 kg	12 lb
150 g	5 oz	675 g	1½ lb	5 kg	13 lb
165 g	5½ oz	900 g	2 lb	6.5 kg	14 lb
175 g	6 oz	1.25 kg	2½–2¾ lb	6.75 kg	15 lb
185 g	6½ oz	1.5 kg	3–3½ lb		

The microwave is a boon in the kitchen and can be used on its own to produce plain and fancy dishes. Food cooks quickly and more healthily, a very important factor in the modern diet.

Precious vitamins are retained because less water is needed. Salt is kept to the minimum as the smaller amount of water requires less salt, so consequently natural flavours are stronger. Microwaves make very little use of fat and, since frying is neither permitted nor safe, the microwave diet is much better for you. As roasts cook, the melted fat oozes out and can be spooned away straightaway. Colours remain true – brown tinged cabbage, lifeless carrots and drab looking beans do not feature in the microwave diet.

The microwave copes well too with convenience foods, but they may contain additives to preserve and increase their shelf life and are therefore not so healthy. A better performance is achieved when using the microwave for home cooking that is based on prime ingredients. Textures remain crisp and food retains its shape. Vegetables taste infinitely superior, rice grains will remain separate, and stewed fruit need not be mushy.

The microwave will defrost, reheat and cook – it can also be used for heating small quantities; for example, when only a cup of water or milk is needed. You can save on washing-up bowls and saucepans by using the microwave for melting gelatine and chocolate, for drying herbs, warming jams, freshening hardened sugar, blanching vegetables, softening butter and making rusks. Some of these functions can save you a lot of time – for instance, if citrus fruit is slightly warmed, the juices will squeeze much more easily.

As microwave cooking is for most people a new form of cooking it must be understood if you wish to make the best use of it. Traditional cooking is a combination of art and science and needs some technical skill. Although professional cooks and dedicated amateurs produce the finest dishes, there are very few people who cannot cook at all. Everyone will have had a few lessons or guidance, or at most have seen their mother or father prepare food at home. But who has ever been taught microwave cooking at home? It is a relatively new discovery and the methods are completely different from any other. You may be able to go to classes – I have been teaching the subject for several years – and although this is the easiest way to learn, you can 'teach-yourself'. In Chapter 5 I will take you through basics from the beginning and it is worth spending a little time to master these.

Although microwaving is a totally different form of cooking, the attention it requires is almost as great as when cooking in the old-fashioned way. You have to stir frequently but not constantly, reposition when necessary, and judge when food is cooked by looking and testing. Do not leave it to its own devices.

To make the most of the microwave, use it for defrosting and reheating, for cooking the foods it is best at, and for helping to prepare the component parts of simple or more complicated dishes. Used in conjunction with the regular oven and grill, you will be able to speed up the cooking process, while still achieving perfect results.

The combination of your microwave oven with the conventional cooker will enable you to reap the benefit of faster, cleaner, tastier cooking, together with browning in the way you have always been used to.

CHOOSING AND USING
MICROWAVE OVENS

Microwaves and combination ovens have so many different features that choosing the right oven for your needs can be very confusing. The following guidelines should be of help.

WHAT TO BUY

If you are not already a microwave owner, you may be having difficulty in choosing which of the vast selection of models available is the most suitable for you. Before you set foot in the shop, give some thought to what you are going to use your microwave for; in other words, what do you expect your microwave to do for you? The following questions will help you make your decision.

1. How many people are you going to cook for?
2. What is your lifestyle – for example, are you at home all day or do you have to come in from work and cook a rushed meal in the evening?
3. Are you going to use the microwave simply for defrosting and reheating or are you going to cook with it? You may be surprised at the amount you will do when the microwave grows on you.
4. With other people in your household be using the microwave? If so, choose either a simple one or a microwave with pre-set programmes.
5. Do you prefer touch control (the advantage of this is that cleaning is so much easier)?
6. Do you fully understand the difference between a turntable model and one with a rectangular base plate?
7. You will have heard about combination ovens, but did you know that there are several different types? Look into this before buying as you may find a simple microwave is still your best choice.
8. How much do you wish to spend?
9. Do you anticipate buying a second microwave later on, and are you likely to use your microwave in other homes – for example, a country cottage?
10. Where are you going to site your microwave – do you require a built-in or a free-standing model?
11. Make sure you understand the differences in microwave ratings: for example, a 500-watt oven will be about one-fifth slower than a 700-watt output oven.
12. Are you really going to need ten settings, and will you make use of delay starts? Will automatic cooking be a great convenience to you and, if this is the case, remember that automatic cooking is described in different ways?

Next consider the dimensions of the oven that you are proposing to buy. Some are wider than others, some are longer, and some are taller. So it may be advisable to take a tape measure along to the shop. The internal dimensions are often as important as the external, since you cannot put a very tall pot in a shallow oven and it is sometimes difficult to stir mixtures while they are in the oven if there is insufficient height to insert a wooden spoon during cooking.

Other points to be considered are venting, as every oven has to be vented. If you are an untidy family and are likely to put books and magazines on top of the oven, then it is far better to buy a microwave that vents at the back or the side. Remember that you must allow about 5 cm/2 inches space around the oven for air circulation.

Prices vary considerably and it is a good idea to shop around. Some of the microwave magazines list current recommended prices and it is usually possible to find a retailer who offers discount. Sometimes last year's model will be selling at a lower price and, although the fascia may be somewhat out of date, the microwave performance will be just as good as if you had bought a new model

TYPES OF MICROWAVES

At the top end of the market are combination ovens incorporating a fan-assisted, thermostatically controlled conventional oven, combined with variable microwave power plus a grill. A double hot plate is additionally built into the top. In between are numerous different models made the more complicated by choices of colour. If you are going in for a sophisticated oven, you must be prepared to spend some time studying the handbook as, unfortunately, these are not always very clearly written. The best way to learn how to use the oven is to stand with the book in one hand and operate the controls with the other. With practice, you will soon find yourself setting it without thinking.

FEATURES

Advertising blurb and leaflets always go on about features – so what are these features and how important are they?

Mode Stirrer or Rotating Antenna

This is simply a fan that revolves to help distribute the microwaves evenly throughout the cabinet. Its purpose is to break up the microwaves, making them work harder. All microwave ovens have some method of doing this and they are equally effective, so you can ignore this point if you wish.

Turntable

Any moving object in the microwave will aid even cooking, but since all ovens are fitted with some device for this purpose (see the paragraph above), you should not buy an oven with a turntable for this reason alone.

A turntable is useful because a) it catches spillage, b) it can be removed for easy cleaning and c) food can be cooked directly on it. Although space may seem limited on the turntable, there is little microwave activity in the corners of the oven, so the turntable covers the areas of maximum microwave activity.

Models without a turntable do, however, give equally good results. Larger dishes can be used, but if they are to be turned, remember that the interior of the microwave is rectangular so that dishes of a similar shape can only be fitted in one direction.

Shelves

These are likely to be metal racks that can be inserted in the middle of the oven, thus giving more available space. In practice, shelves can be a nuisance because much thought has to be put in to which foods should go where as the top section in the oven is 'hotter' in microwave terms. Should the cavity be filled with dishes, the cooking times will be much slower.

Temperature Probe

This is a sort of uncalibrated thermometer; one end is inserted into a small aperture in the ceiling or cabinet lining and the pointed solid end is put into the food. When the food reaches the required internal temperature, the current automatically switches off. This is a useful device if you are poor at judging cooking times. Probes sometimes make mistakes because an even temperature throughout the item is hard to achieve.

Auto Sensor

The auto sensor is built into the oven 'works' and is not visible to the naked eye. It can work in two different ways, depending on the manufacturer's design. In one type of microwave, the auto sensor detects humidity as vapour escapes, and the other kind senses an increase in the temperature inside the cavity due to steam being driven off the food. They both then determine automatically how long cooking will take.

Microwaves fitted with an auto sensor are generally reliable and can be adjusted to suit the 'doneness' required. Cooking usually takes longer, but there is an advantage in that you do not have to 'watch the pot'.

Programmable Memory

You can either pre-set cooking times yourself so that if you use the same recipe regularly you only have to touch the control to register that usual cooking time, or on some models, you dial in the weight of the food and the cooking time is automatically calculated. Other ovens have a larger number of pre-set, built-in timings.

Delay Start

This is very similar to setting a conventional automatic oven; machines with a delay start can be programmed to Defrost/Pause/Cook and there are other permutations of these functions.

Power Settings

These are sometimes measured in percentages and sometimes stated numerically 1 to 10. Two, three or more fixed settings up to Full Power may be clicked into position on a revolving switch or marked in various ways on indicated panels such as Defrost/Medium/Roast/Simmer. These speeds are roughly equivalent to conventional calibration. It is convenient to be able to adjust these speeds, but there is little difference between any two positions. At the cheaper end of the scale are microwaves with two power settings (Full and Defrost), and a maximum output of 500 watts. If time is of the essence, choose a model rated 600, 650 or 700 watts; the highest wattage being the fastest.

WHAT DISHES TO USE

Ovenproof glass, ceramics, stoneware, some plastics and paper are all microwave suitable. Specially designed bakeware can also be used up to 200°C/400°F/Gas Mark 6 in the conventional oven. Stoneware, ceramics and ovenglass are resistant to slightly higher temperatures. Only Corning ware can be used additionally on the hob and under the grill. Metal must not be used in the microwave, but can in some instances be used in a combination oven (check in the handbook that comes with the model you have purchased). For further details of appropriate cookware, see Chapter 5.

HOW TO CLEAN THE MICROWAVE

The microwave must be kept scrupulously clean if it is to be effective and safe to use. Wipe over with a damp cloth moistened with washing-up liquid. Combination ovens must be treated more carefully, as scouring will damage the microwave linings.

A combination oven may consist of: a] microwave/grill b] microwave/fan oven c] microwave/radiant browning d] microwave/top browning convection e] microwave/convection/grill f] microwave/convection/grill/hob. In most, it is possible to use the methods simultaneously. In others they can only be used consecutively. Consecutive cooking is similar to combination cookery as outlined in Chapter 3.

The main aim of a combination oven is to achieve a reasonable degree of brownness and doneness in the shortest possible time. Since microwaving is so much quicker than conventional baking, it can happen that cakes and pies are either cooked but too pale, or become an acceptable brown colour but be overcooked inside or even ruined. Joints may have a tough, overcooked outside yet be raw in the middle, and casseroles may become dry around the outer edges. To be sure that even results are obtained using both types of cooking, the microwave power must be reduced, especially when the conventional cooking period is likely to be lengthy. To resolve the problem in some of their recipes, manufacturers call for the drastically reduced 10 per cent microwave power setting. This means that the microwaves are at warming level only, which is so low as to be almost useless. The majority of combination ovens are pre-set at what is generally understood as Defrost level, which is approximately 35 per cent of Full Power. These levels however vary in intensity too and the recipes in this chapter should give satisfactory results on Defrost ratings varying between 180 and 230 watts. It is possible you may have to adjust times even within this bracket.

As a general rule, if you want to convert recipes that have been written for conventional cookery – this is nothing to do with translating manufacturer's recipes one to another – raise the temperature, reduce the cooking time by one-third and couple a high temperature setting with microwave power at Defrost (35 per cent). There is an advantage in preheating the oven, although not all manufacturers recommend this.

The combination oven is to be recommended for defrosting and reheating ready-prepared convenience foods. The dry heat in the cabinet combined with the microwave mode will speed up the process and the results will be what you would expect to find when using just conventional methods. When a combination oven is used for microwave alone, microwaving will be slower due to a lack of space between the bottom of the dish and the metal turntable or oven base. This will impede the reflection of microwaves. I therefore find it better to raise those dishes containing foods that do not need to be stirred. When cooking in a dual oven, it is often a good idea to do the same thing. Whatever you use to separate the dish from the base of the oven, it must be made of material through which the microwaves can pass.

Not all containers that are suitable for the microwave are suitable for the combination oven. Bakeware for dual use must be extremely heat resistant, but at the same time must not impede the microwaves and, when purchasing, look for containers that are suitably labelled. Combination ovens must not be scratched or scoured by using rough cleansing pads or gritty powders; they must be treated more gently.

COMBINATION
COOKING

FRENCH ONION SOUP

For a better flavour, store the ungarnished soup in a cool place for 24 hours before reheating, and cook the croûtons at this time.

SERVES 4

◆

450 g/1 lb large onions
30 g/1 oz butter
1 teaspoon flour
1 litre/1¾ pints boiling water
1 chicken stock cube
140 ml/¼ pint dry red wine
1 teaspoon red wine vinegar
1 teaspoon tomato purée
½ teaspoon dried rosemary
3 tablespoons grated Parmesan cheese
Salt and freshly milled black pepper
A little extra butter
1 × 2.5 cm/1 inch slice bread

◆

Set the combination oven at 250°C. Peel and slice the onions into rings. Reserve one strip of onion skin. Put the onions, skin and butter in a deep roasting dish. Without covering, cook, stirring occasionally, until the onions are just beginning to brown (about 10 minutes). Stir in the flour and cook for about 5 minutes. Mix in the water, crumbled stock cube, wine, vinegar, tomato purée, rosemary and 1 tablespoon of grated Parmesan. Season with salt and pepper. Without covering, cook until the soup thickens and the liquid is reduced by one-third (about 15 minutes). Cover and set aside.

Butter the bread on both sides, put on non-stick baking parchment and cook in the hot combination oven until brown and crisp (about 2 minutes). Cut into quarters. Sprinkle with the remaining Parmesan and return to the combination oven. Without covering, cook to melt the cheese (about 2 minutes).

Remove the onion skin from the soup. Adjust the seasoning and, without covering, reheat the soup (about 3 minutes). Float the bread on the surface and cook for a further minute. Serve at once.

TOAD-IN-THE-HOLE

Toad-in-the-hole cannot be cooked by microwave alone, but when cooked in the combination oven it is a huge success.

SERVES 4 to 6

◆

140 g/5 oz plain flour
Pinch of salt
2 large eggs
285 ml/½ pint milk
Margarine, lard or oil for greasing
450 g/1 lb beef or pork sausages

◆

Sift the flour and salt into a mixing bowl and make a well in the centre. Beat the eggs and milk together. Pour into the well and gradually work in the flour, beating continuously to avoid lumps forming.

Set the combination oven at 250°C. Grease a deep ovenglass roasting dish. Prick the sausages and arrange in the dish in a single layer. Place the dish of sausages in the oven during conventional preheating. When the oven is hot, pour the batter over the sausages. Without covering, cook on combination until the batter has risen and is brown around the sides and the sausages are cooked (about 40 minutes).

ROAST CHICKEN

The combination oven is great for roasting poultry: cooking is fast, the flesh is tender, and there is a crisp golden skin. You must make sure that the bird is not too big to fit into the cavity.

SERVES 4 to 5

❖

1.5-1.8 kg/3½-4 lb chicken, fully thawed
Salt and pepper
1 onion (optional)
Butter or oil

❖

Set the combination oven at 250°C. Rinse and pat the chicken dry with kitchen paper. Place on a ceramic roasting rack in a shallow ovenglass dish or cook directly on the rack or perforated tray, according to the manufacturer's handbook. Season the chicken inside with salt and pepper, inserting the whole onion for extra flavour. Rub the outside of the skin with butter or oil.

Cover the chicken with a slit roasting bag. Cook for about 30-40 minutes, depending on the weight. Leave for 10 minutes before uncovering and testing.

ROAST BEEF

Timings on roasts depend on the weight and shape of the joint. To be sure that the meat is cooked to your liking, you must test with a meat thermometer. The centre of the joint is the last to cook. After the recommended cooking time, tent the meat with foil and leave to stand for 10 minutes to enable even heat to diffuse, disperse and spread. Test with the meat thermometer and give additional time if necessary. You can only use a combination oven for joints weighing more than 1.5 kg/3 lb. Allow 18-20 minutes per 450 g/1 lb for medium done, plus an additional 10 minutes per joint.

SERVES 8 to 10

❖

1.8 kg/4 lb joint beef
Gravy browning

❖

Set the combination oven at 200°C. Place the joint on a ceramic rack in an ovenglass roasting dish and cook for about 1 hour for rare meat, turning the joint over halfway through cooking. Remove the rack and joint from the dish, baste away the fat and thicken the juices with gravy browning. Allow to heat through for about 5 minutes. Serve separately with the carved meat.

Note: Roast pork, which must be thoroughly cooked, requires 12-16 minutes per 450 g/1 lb. Roast lamb requires 20 minutes per 450 g/1 lb.

	Temperature before standing	Temperature after standing
Rare	50°C/120°F	60°C/140°F
Medium	55°C/130°F	70°C/160°F
Well done	70°C/160°F	75°C/170°F

HUNGARIAN GOULYAS

Make sure you use the sweet and not the hot paprika, which is too pungent.

SERVES 5 to 6

❖

675 g/1½ lb lean raw beef
2 large onions
1 stick celery
450 g/1 lb potatoes
45 g/1½ oz butter
1 tablespoon sweet paprika
1 tablespoon flour
Salt and freshly milled black pepper
1 × 395 g/14 oz can tomatoes, chopped

❖

Set the combination oven at 220°C. Cut the meat into 2 cm/¾ inch cubes. Thinly slice the onions and celery. Peel and cut the potatoes into chunks. Put the butter in a large casserole with the onions and celery and stir in the paprika. Cook until the onions are soft and golden (about 10 minutes).

Stir in the flour and beef and season with salt and pepper. Add the potatoes and stir in the tomatoes. Cover with the lid and cook, stirring once during cooking, until the meat is tender (about 15 minutes).

Serve on a bed of rice with French beans or a green salad.

ALBINSSON'S TEMPTATION

Here shredded potatoes and sliced onions are baked in a tomato and cream sauce which is fully absorbed during the cooking.

SERVES 4 to 6

◆

675 g/1½ lb potatoes
2 large onions
6 sprigs dill weed
½ teaspoon celery salt
3 tablespoons tomato purée
140 ml/¼ pint double cream
2 tablespoons dried breadcrumbs
15 g/½ oz butter

◆

Set the combination oven at 200°C. Thinly peel, then shred the potatoes by hand or grate coarsely in a food processor. Thinly slice the onions. Discard the stems and chop the dill weed finely. Sprinkle the celery salt over the potatoes and stir to mix. Grease a 20 cm/8 inch round by 4 cm/1½ inch deep ovenproof dish. Arrange thin layers of potatoes, onions and dill weed, finishing with potatoes. Blend the tomato purée with the cream. Pour over the potatoes. Top with the breadcrumbs and dab with butter.

Cook in the hot oven until the vegetables are tender and the crust is golden brown (about 25 minutes).

Roast Chicken (*see page 17*) and Albinsson's Temptation

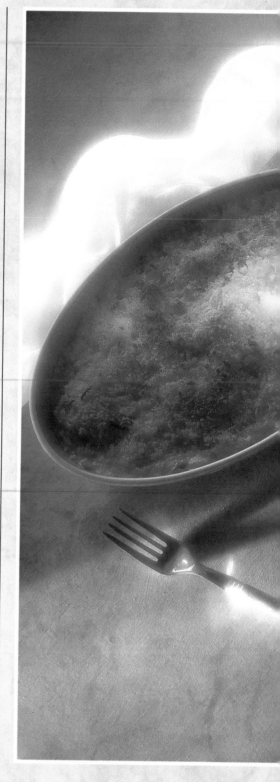

STEAK AND KIDNEY PIE

Remember to cut the beef into really small pieces to be sure it is well cooked yet soft.

SERVES 4 to 6

❖

Pastry
225 g/8 oz flour
1 teaspoon salt
170 g/6 oz butter
2 teaspoons lemon juice
7 tablespoons iced water
Filling
450 g/1 lb lean beef
3 lamb's kidneys
Salt and freshly milled black pepper
2 tablespoons flour
2 tablespoons oil
1 onion, finely chopped
285 ml/½ pint hot water
Dash of Worcestershire sauce
1 beef stock cube
1 egg, beaten

❖

To make the pastry, sieve the flour and salt into a mixing bowl. Divide the butter into four pieces and rub in one-quarter. Mix the lemon juice with the water, pour into the flour all at once and mix with a round-bladed knife to a soft elastic dough. Add more water if needed. Knead until smooth on a floured surface. Refrigerate for 10 minutes.

Roll out the pastry to a rectangle three times as long as it is wide. Using one-quarter of the butter, cover two-thirds of the strip with butter pieces, leaving a 1 cm/½ inch border. Fold the plain section over one buttered section and fold the remaining buttered section over that. Seal the edges with a rolling pin. Give the pastry a quarter turn, roll out again and spread one-quarter of the butter in dabs over two-thirds of the surface. Fold, seal and turn. Roll out and cover with the remaining butter as before. Fold, roll out and fold again. Wrap in cling film and leave in the refrigerator for 1 hour.

Meanwhile, set the combination oven at 200°C. Cut the meat into small pieces. Skin, core and slice the kidneys, season with salt and pepper and toss in the flour. Put the oil in a large ovenglass pie dish and heat until hot (about 2 minutes). Stir in the beef cubes and onion and, without

covering, cook until slightly browned (about 5 minutes). Pour in the water and Worcestershire sauce and crumble in the stock cube. Without covering, cook until beginning to thicken (about 10 minutes). Remove from the oven and leave to cool for 15 minutes.

Roll out the pastry to 5 mm/¼ inch thickness and to the shape of the dish with a 1 cm/½ inch border all round. Without stretching, place over the meat, dampening the edges of the dish. Press to seal, trim the edges and make a hole with a skewer to enable the steam to escape. Brush the pastry with beaten egg, then bake until the pastry crust is golden (about 40 minutes).

TARTE TATIN

This recipe originates from France where Tarte Tatin appears as regularly for a dessert as our apple pie.

SERVES 5 to 6

❖

Pastry
115 g/4 oz flour
Pinch of salt
85 g/3 oz hard margarine
1-1½ tablespoons cold water
Filling
45 g/1½ oz butter
85 g/3 oz caster sugar
900 g/2 lb small cooking apples
1 tablespoon Calvados or Brandy

❖

To make the pastry, sieve the flour and salt into a mixing bowl. Grate in the margarine, stir, then add enough cold water to make a firm but not stiff dough. Roll out on a floured surface to a 25 cm/10 inch diameter circle. Refrigerate while preparing the filling. Set the combination oven at 200°C.

To make the filling, put the butter in a deep 23 cm/9 inch diameter ovenglass cake dish. Without covering, heat until melted (about 30 seconds). Stir in the sugar and, without covering, cook until light brown and caramelized (2 minutes).

Peel, core and quarter the apples. Arrange the apple pieces around the sides and in the centre of the dish. Cover with the pastry lid, tucking the edge in around the inside of the dish. Cook until the pastry is crisp but not brown (about 30 minutes). Turn out onto a heated flameproof dish. Switch off the oven.

Put the Calvados in a small ovenproof bowl and, without covering, heat on Full Power for no more than 15 seconds – take care as the bowl will be very hot. Pour over the apples and immediately ignite.

BREAD AND BUTTER PUDDING

Wholemeal bread and golden granulated sugar together with nutritious eggs and milk make this pudding suitable for young and old.

SERVES 6

❖

6 slices wholemeal bread, buttered
85 g/3 oz sultanas
30 g/1 oz chopped mixed peel
55 g/2 oz golden granulated sugar
450 ml/¾ pint milk
3 eggs
½ teaspoon grated nutmeg

❖

Cut each slice of bread into four triangles. Grease an oval pie dish and line the base and sides with half the bread, buttered side up. Sprinkle with the sultanas and peel and half the sugar. Cover with the remaining bread, buttered side up, and sprinkle with the remaining sugar.

Put the milk in a jug and, without covering, heat on Full Power until warm (about 1 minute). Beat in the eggs. Strain over the bread and leave to soak for 30 minutes. Sprinkle with the nutmeg.

Set the combination oven at 180°C. Without covering, bake in the oven until set and lightly brown (about 20 minutes).

TELFORD THINS

These light, thin, crispy biscuits have a lemony flavour and are ideal to serve with morning coffee.

MAKES 12 to 16

◆

55 g//2 oz butter
55 g/2 oz caster sugar
115 g/4 oz plain flour
1 egg yolk
1 teaspoon grated lemon rind
Icing sugar

◆

Cream the butter and caster sugar until fluffy. Stir in 1 tablespoon of flour. Beat the egg yolk and stir in gradually, then mix in the lemon rind and remaining flour. Alternatively, mix all the ingredients together in the food processor. Form into a ball and chill until firm (30 minutes).

Set the combination oven at 180-200°C. Roll out on a floured surface to 3 mm/⅛ inch thickness. Cut out twelve 5-7.5 cm/2-2½ inch round biscuits. Spread out six or eight at a time on a baking tray that will fit the oven or turntable and cook until pale beige (about 6 minutes). Remove while warm with a palette knife and sprinkle with icing sugar. Cook the remaining batch in the same way.

Store the cooked biscuits in an airtight container.

**Crunchy Lemon Drizzle Cake (*see page 24*) and
Telford Thins**

CRUNCHY LEMON DRIZZLE CAKE

Serve warm as a dessert with stewed fruit and yogurt or cold as a cake. On cooling, the cake develops a crunchy crust.

SERVES 6 to 8

◆

115 g/4 oz butter
140 g/5 oz caster sugar
2 large eggs
Grated rind and juice of 1 lemon
170 g/6 oz self-raising flour
70 g/2½ oz icing sugar
1 tablespoon lemon juice
To decorate
Lemon slices and mimosa balls

◆

Set the combination oven at 180°C. Grease and base line a 1.5 litre/2½ pint loaf dish. Beat the butter and sugar in a mixing bowl until fluffy. Beat the eggs and lemon rind together. Gradually work into the creamed mixture, beating well after each addition. Sift the flour over the surface, then fold in thoroughly. Stir in 1 tablespoon of lemon juice. Spoon into the prepared dish. Cook in the preheated oven until golden brown and just resilient to the touch (about 15 minutes).

Turn the cake out onto a wire rack placed over a clean tray. Blend 2 tablespoons of lemon juice with 55 g/2 oz of the icing sugar in a small ovenglass bowl. Reset the oven to microwave only setting Defrost (35%) and heat for about 30 seconds. Stir until the sugar has dissolved. Remove with ovengloves. Pierce the warm cake deeply all over with a skewer and spoon half the syrup over the top. When it is absorbed, reverse the cake, pierce and add the remaining syrup. Turn over and sprinkle with the remaining icing sugar. Decorate with lemon slices and mimosa balls.

PEACH CRUMBLE

For a quick method of making the topping, finely chop the dry ingredients together in a food processor. Add the margarine and 'pulse' until mixed to fine breadcrumbs.

SERVES 4 to 5

◆

1 × 425 g/15 oz can sliced peaches
85 g/3 oz porridge oats
140 g/5 oz plain flour
2 teaspoons mixed spice
Pinch of salt
115 g/4 oz soft margarine
115 g/4 oz demerara sugar
1 tablespoon chopped, skinned pistachio nuts

◆

Drain the peaches and reserve the juice. Set six peach slices aside for decoration and spread the remainder in a lightly greased 20 cm/8 inch round ovenproof dish. Mix the oats, flour, spice and salt together. Rub in the margarine, then stir in the sugar. Spoon the mixture over the peaches and press down lightly. Arrange the reserved peach slices in a spoke design.

Set the combination oven at 220°C. Without covering, cook until golden brown (about 15 minutes). Sprinkle with the chopped pistachios before serving.

If liked, heat the juice in a jug (about 1½ minutes) and pour over the crumble portions when serving.

ALMOND AND CHERRY MADEIRA CAKE

This cake is best eaten on the day it is baked. To prevent it drying out, wrap the cake in cling film or foil after it has cooled.

SERVES 6 to 7

◆

**3 eggs
1 teaspoon vanilla essence
170 g/6 oz soft margarine
170 g/6 oz caster sugar
200 g/7 oz self-raising flour
1 teaspoon baking powder
2 tablespoons milk
30 g/1 oz flaked almonds
5 glacé cherries, chopped**

◆

Set the combination oven at 200°C. Grease an 18 cm/7 inch straight-sided, glass soufflé dish and place a disc of non-stick baking parchment in the base. Beat the eggs, vanilla essence, margarine, caster sugar, flour and baking powder together for 2 minutes. Stir in the milk, then fold in the almonds. Turn the mixture into the dish and smooth the top, then make a slight indentation in the centre of the cake with the underside of a tablespoon.

Cook in the centre of the preheated oven until the cake is risen but still pale (about 15 minutes). Quickly sprinkle the cherries over the surface, then continue cooking until light brown (about 10 minutes). Test with a skewer and, if the mixture is insufficiently cooked, reduce the temperature to 180°C and continue cooking for a further 3-4 minutes. Leave for 5 minutes before removing the cake from the dish. Cool on a wire rack.

SULTANA FRUIT CAKE

This light fruit cake is delicious when freshly baked. Sliced stale fruit cake can be gently reheated on Defrost and served with custard for a quick pudding.

SERVES 8

◆

**115 g/4 oz soft margarine
115 g/4 oz dark soft brown sugar
225 g/8 oz plain flour
1 teaspoon baking powder
30 g/1 oz ground almonds
3 eggs
2 tablespoons milk
¼ teaspoon almond essence
225 g/8 oz sultanas
10-15 flaked almonds**

◆

Grease an 18 cm/7 inch straight-sided, glass soufflé dish and place a disc of non-stick baking parchment in the base. Set the combination oven at 200°C.

Beat the margarine and sugar together until light and fluffy. Mix the flour, baking powder and ground almonds together, then gradually stir into the mixture. Beat the eggs with the milk and almond essence, add to the bowl and mix well. Fold in the sultanas. Turn the mixture into the dish and smooth the top. Sprinkle with flaked almonds.

Cook in the centre of the preheated oven until the cake is brown and a skewer inserted near the centre comes out clean (about 15 minutes). Remove from the cake dish and serve warm. To prevent the cake becoming stale, wrap it in foil.

For some people cooking is a 'grande experience' and indeed for many it is an enjoyable hobby, but when you have to prepare daily meals, the task can be both onerous and monotonous. It is easy to sit down and eat a meal that someone else has prepared without fully appreciating just how much effort has gone into preparing the food.

The arrival of the microwave on the domestic scene has proved a considerable help for cooks. It is excellent for cooking all foods that do not need browning and can replace a saucepan for steaming, boiling and simmering. You should make the most of its defrosting and reheating capabilities and use it for melting, softening and heating small quantities. It is also unsurpassed for cooking vegetables, fish (other than fried), sauces, custards, jams and jellies. There are, however, limitations in its abilities. It cannot be used for any kind of frying – for example, breaded fish, and pancakes – and top surface browning is impossible, so roast chicken remains pale, pork has no crispy crackling, potato-topped pies stay white, and cakes will not brown. Food cooked by microwave alone must either be soft or completely crisp throughout; it is not possible to achieve a crusty, crispy outside and a soft interior.

In most recipes there are parts that can be more easily prepared by microwave and others that lend themselves to other cooking methods. Traditional appliances, including the frying pan, grill, hob and conventional oven, when assisted by the microwave will enable you to bring a wider variety of dishes to your table.

In this chapter I have planned the recipes in what I think is the most effective and economical way. For example, in one recipe I may suggest boiling potatoes in a saucepan, yet in another recommend cooking them in the microwave. The methods are equally good, but my intention is to avoid wasting time, while waiting for one component part to cook – you can use whichever method you prefer. However, you can use these recipes either in a combination oven or using a separate microwave and conventional oven, but not all combination ovens are fitted with a grill, and frying is always a separate process. If you are using the combination oven, you cannot cook component parts simultaneously. Take care when alternating between microwave and conventional cooking – oven gloves are essential as the oven will be hot after using it for conventional baking. Do not use ordinary microwave plastic dishes unless they are heat resistant.

Most family dishes regularly appear in cookery books, but the selection of ordinary, everyday recipes in this chapter have a slightly unusual approach. In addition, I have included some more upmarket dishes that are suitable for entertaining. All are relatively easy to prepare with the combined use of microwave and other cooking methods.

Choose cooking utensils and bake ware that can be transferred from one type of cooking appliance to the other, bearing in mind that metal is not suitable in the microwave and few plastics can go into a conventional oven, especially at high temperatures. Corning ware and ovenproof glass are good choices, but only Corning ware is suitable under the grill.

As time goes by and more and more households have a microwave and when the microwave novelty is over, we will revert to the most sensible way of cooking regardless of the appliance.

COMBINING MICROWAVE
AND CONVENTIONAL
COOKING

SMOKED KIPPER FLAN

If kipper does not suit your palate, you can try using smoked haddock instead. This also works well as a starter.

SERVES 5 to 6

◆

285 g/10 oz ready-to-roll shortcrust pastry
340 g/12 oz kipper fillets
milk
45 g/1½ oz butter
140 ml/¼ pint water
70 g/2½ oz flour
Pinch of salt
2 large eggs
Sprigs of parsley
Slices of lemon
Sauce
55 g/2 oz butter
15 g/½ oz flour
Freshly milled black pepper
2 tablespoons double cream
115 g/4 oz Leicester cheese, grated

◆

Roll out the pastry on a floured surface to a 30 cm/12 inch circle. Place a 23 cm/9 inch flan ring in the centre of a greased baking tray and put in the pastry, pressing it well into the corners and allowing 5 mm/¼ inch above the rim. Flute the edges. Chill.

▲▲ Arrange the kipper fillets in a shallow dish in two layers separated by greaseproof paper. Cover again with greaseproof paper and cook on Full Power until the edges curl up (about 2 minutes). Remove the skin and any stray bones. Set fish aside. Pour the juices into a measuring jug and make up to 285 ml/½ pint with milk. Reserve for the sauce.

Put the butter and water in a medium bowl and, without covering, cook on Full Power until bubbles appear around the edges (about 2 minutes). Continue cooking until the water rises up the sides of the bowl. Immediately tip in the flour mixed with the salt. Beat thoroughly. Replace in the microwave and, without covering, cook for 30 seconds. Beat again, then beat in the eggs one at a time, stirring vigorously between each addition.

Put into a piping bag fitted with a plain 1 cm/½ inch nozzle. Leave to cool. Pipe a thick circle of choux paste around the inside edge of the pastry base. Using a slotted spoon, fill the centre with the kipper fillets.

▲▲ To make the sauce, put the butter in a medium bowl. Without covering, heat on Full Power until melted (about 30 seconds). Stir in the flour. Add the fish and milk liquor and mix with a wire whisk. Without covering, cook, stirring frequently, until the sauce thickens (about 2½ minutes). Season with pepper and stir in the cream. Mix in three-quarters of the cheese and pour the sauce over the kippers.

◀ Pipe the remaining choux paste carefully over the sauce, holding the piping bag horizontally, but above the sauce. Make sure the choux paste touches the sides of the pastry case. Brush with milk and sprinkle with the remaining cheese. Bake in a preheated 220°C/425°F/Gas Mark 7 oven until risen and golden brown (about 45 minutes).

Run a table knife between the pastry and the flan ring and carefully lift off the ring. Transfer the flan to a heated serving dish, using two fish slices. Serve hot garnished with sprigs of parsley and thinly-sliced lemon.

STIR-FRIED HADDOCK WITH PRAWN SAUCE

Judge this dish by the superb flavour and texture for the appearance is somewhat bland.

SERVES 4 to 5

◆

800 g/1¾ lb fresh haddock fillet
Salt and pepper
1 tablespoon lemon juice
1 tablespoon dry vermouth
Sauce
1 medium onion
2 tablespoons salad oil
30 g/1 oz flour
425 ml/¾ pint milk
170 g/6 oz peeled cooked prawns
¼ teaspoon anchovy essence
Salt and pepper
To complete
2 tablespoons salad oil
225/8 oz freshly cooked egg noodles

◆

Skin the haddock and cut the fish into 2.5 cm/1 inch cubes. Season with salt and pepper. Put in a bowl and add the lemon juice and vermouth. Stir gently, cover and set aside.

▲▲ To make the sauce, put the onion in a cereal bowl and cover with a saucer. Cook on Full Power to soften (about 2 minutes), then cut into quarters. Put the onion and all the other sauce ingredients in a food processor and blend to a purée. Pour into a large bowl and, without covering, cook, stirring occasionally, until the sauce thickens (about 4 minutes). Taste and adjust the seasoning.

◀ Heat the oil in a frying pan until hazy. Add the fish, a few pieces at a time, turning gently to cook all sides.

Serve the fish on cooked egg noodles and mask with the prawn sauce.

SEA FOOD GRATIN

This looks most attractive when served as the pink prawns show through the lightly-speckled brown top.

SERVES 6

◆

680 g/1½ lb fresh cod or haddock fillet
¼ onion
6 peppercorns
1 bay leaf
2 sprigs parsley
285 ml/½ pint milk
Salt and pepper
1 tablespoon lemon juice
115 g/4 oz button mushrooms
170 g/6 oz peeled cooked prawns
30 g/1 oz butter
30 g/1 oz flour
2 tablespoons mayonnaise
1 tablespoon grated Parmesan cheese

◆

▲▲ Skin the fish. Roughly cut up the skins and put them in a medium bowl with the onion, peppercorns, bay leaf and parsley. Add the milk and heat on Full Power, without covering, until steaming but not boiling (about 3 minutes). Cover and set aside to infuse for about 30 minutes.

Meanwhile, cut the fish into chunks, season with salt and pepper and sprinkle with lemon juice. Put into a shallow oval pie dish. Quarter the mushrooms and arrange with the prawns on top of the fish.

Put the butter in a medium bowl and, without covering, heat on Full Power until melted (about 45 seconds). Stir in the flour and cook until the paste begins to dry (about 30 seconds). Strain in the infused milk and stir with a wire whisk. Without covering, cook, stirring occasionally, until the sauce thickens (about 1½ minutes). Stir in the mayonnaise. Season with salt and pepper.

Without covering, cook the dish of fish until the white fish is flaky (about 7 minutes). Spoon out excess liquor and mix with the sauce. Pour the sauce over the mushroom and prawn topping and sprinkle with the cheese.

◀ Set the grill on high, and put the dish at a 10 cm/4 inch distance below the grill until brown.

CRAB AND LIME STUFFED BASS

This is an example of how the less common fish that are readily available can be easily cooked and attractively served.

SERVES 6 to 7

◆

1 bunch spring onions
1 medium green pepper
1 clove garlic
2 tomatoes
30 g/1 oz butter
2 tablespoons freshly-squeezed lime juice from 1 lime
170 g/6 oz flaked canned crabmeat
2 tablespoons medium white wine
Salt and freshly milled black pepper
1 × 1.6 kg/3½ lb sea bass
Garnish
1 fresh lime, sliced

◆

▲▲ Trim and finely slice the onions. Core, de-seed and chop the green pepper. Peel and crush the garlic. Skin, quarter, de-seed and chop the tomatoes. Put the onions, chopped pepper and garlic in a large bowl. Add the butter, cover and cook on Full Power, stirring occasionally, until the vegetables are soft (about 4 minutes). Mix in the tomatoes and lime juice and, without covering, cook until thickened (about 3 minutes). Stir in the crabmeat and wine. Season generously with salt and pepper.

◄ Remove the head of the fish, then slit the skin along the backbone and slide a sharp knife between the flesh and bones to separate the halves. Discard the bones. Lay one half of the fish, cut side up, in the centre of a large sheet of non-stick baking parchment. Spread with the crab and lime filling and place the other half on top. Fold up and pleat the baking parchment around the fish until completely enclosed. Place on a baking tray.

Bake in a preheated 180°C/350°F/Gas Mark 4 oven for about 25 minutes. Open up the baking parchment and cook until the fish flakes easily (about 10 minutes).

Slice a table knife between the skin and the flesh and discard the skin. Flip the fish over and remove the remaining skin. Serve garnished with slices of fresh lime.

Crab and Lime Stuffed Bass

HADDOCK SOUFFLÉ

This is an economical soufflé that uses less eggs than normal and only 225 g/8 oz of fish.

SERVES 4 to 5

◆

3 eggs
30 g/1 oz butter
30 g/1 oz flour
140 ml/¼ pint milk
Pinch of Cayenne pepper
½ teaspoon salt
225 g/8 oz white fish fillet, skinned and de-boned
6 spring onions
3 tablespoons freshly chopped parsley

◆

▲▲   Separate the eggs, putting the whites in a large bowl. Heat the butter in a large bowl on Full Power until melted (about 30 seconds), then stir in the flour. Add the milk, Cayenne pepper and salt and beat with a wire whisk until smooth. Without covering, cook on Full Power, stirring frequently, until the sauce is thick (about 2 minutes). Cover and set aside.

Put the fish on a plate. Top, tail and finely slice the onions and spread over the fish. Cover and cook on Full Power until the fish is opaque (about 2 minutes). Mash with a fork and beat into the sauce. Beat in the egg yolks one at a time, stir in the parsley and leave to cool.

Using grease-free beaters, beat the egg whites to soft peaks. Fold into the fish mixture.

◀   Preheat a conventional oven to 180°C/350°F/Gas Mark 4. Pour the fish mixture into an ungreased 15 cm/ 6 inch soufflé dish. Put the soufflé dish in a baking tin containing 1 cm/½ inch of water. Bake until well risen and brown on top (about 30 minutes). Serve at once.

SCAMPI AND EGG FLAN

This is made with a cheese pastry which is filled with stirred egg and then garnished with deep-fried scampi.

SERVES 6

◆

Pastry
85 g/3 oz hard margarine
170 g/6 oz plain flour
55 g/2 oz Cheddar cheese, grated
2-2½ tablespoons cold water
Filling
12 breaded scampi
3 tomatoes
6 eggs
6 tablespoons milk
Salt and freshly milled black pepper
1 teaspoon grated Parmesan cheese

◆

◀   To make the pastry, rub the margarine into the flour until the mixture resembles fine breadcrumbs. Stir in the cheese and add sufficient water to mix to a smooth dough. Roll out to a 23 cm/9 inch circle and use to line a 23 cm/ 9 inch shallow glass cake dish. Chill for 30 minutes, then bake blind in a preheated 200°C/400°F/Gas Mark 6 oven until golden (about 15 minutes).

Meanwhile, deep-fry the breaded scampi at 185°C/ 360°F until golden. Drain on kitchen paper and keep warm.

▲▲   Slice the tomatoes and spread out on a plate. Without covering, cook on Full Power to soften (about 30 seconds). Beat the eggs and milk in a medium bowl and season with salt and pepper. Without covering, cook on Full Power, stirring frequently with a wire whisk, until the egg thickens slightly (about 3 minutes). Stir in the Parmesan cheese.

Spread the tomato slices in the pastry case, pour the egg mixture on top and scatter with the scampi.

SALMON AND CUCUMBER PIE

This easy-to-prepare creamy pie has a tomato garnish and browned potato topping.

SERVES 6

◆

2 large tomatoes
1 × 257 g/8 oz can salmon or tuna
55 g/2oz butter
30 g/1 oz flour
285 ml/½ pint milk
Salt and pepper
2 tablespoons mayonnaise
¼ cucumber, unpeeled
55 g/2 oz Cheddar cheese
680 g/1½ lb cooked potatoes, mashed (see note)

◆

Slice the tomatoes. Drain the salmon and remove any skin and bones.

▲▲ Put half the butter in a medium bowl and heat on Full Power until melted (about 45 seconds). Stir in the flour and cook until puffy (about 30 seconds). Add the milk, season with salt and pepper and stir with a wire whisk. Without covering, cook, stirring occasionally, until the sauce thickens (about 3 minutes). Stir in the mayonnaise. Flake and add the salmon. Dice and add the cucumber. Put the cheese on an undecorated saucer and heat until just melted (about 20 seconds). Pour into the salmon and mix well. Turn the mixture into a flameproof dish.

Put the mashed potatoes in a bowl and add the remaining butter and, without covering, heat on Full Power until the butter is softened and can be mashed in (about 1½ minutes). Season to taste. Pile the creamed potato over the salmon and flatten slightly with a fork. Garnish with a border of tomato slices and, without covering, reheat the pie (about 2 minutes).

◀ Place under a medium grill until brown.

Note: You can use fresh or reconstituted potato. About 100 g/3½ oz of dried potato powder reconstituted with 835 ml/1½ pints of milk is the equivalent of 680 g/1½ lb of fresh mashed potato.

CRAB THERMIDOR

A luxury gourmet starter or main course which can be made with freshly cooked, thawed or canned crab meat. Drain and reserve the juices and use in place of part of the milk if liked.

SERVES 5

◆

85 g/3 oz Emmenthal cheese
30 g/1 oz strong Cheddar cheese
1 small shallot
2 tablespoons white wine
¼ teaspoon French mustard
285 g/10 oz crab meat
Salt and freshly milled white pepper
40 g/1½ oz soft margarine
¼ teaspoon bay leaf powder
35 g/1½ oz flour
285 ml/½ pink milk
1 egg yolk
2 tablespoons fine breadcrumbs

◆

Grate the cheeses and very finely chop the shallot. Mix the wine and mustard together and stir in the crab meat. Season with salt and pepper, then cover and set aside in a cool place.

▲▲ Stir the shallot, margarine and bay leaf powder together in a medium bowl. Without covering, cook on Full Power until the shallot is soft (about 2 minutes). Stir in the flour and gradually mix in the milk (or milk and crab liquor). Beat in the egg yolk. Without covering, cook on Full Power, stirring occasionally, until the sauce thickens (about 2½ minutes).

Pour the sauce into the crab mixture. Stir in half the cheeses. Divide between five scallop shells or ovenproof ramekins.

◀ Mix the remaining cheese and breadcrumbs together and sprinkle on top. Bake on a baking tray in a pre-heated oven 200°C/400°F/Gas Mark 6 until hot, and brown on top (about 15 minutes).

Serve with green tagliatelli or a mixed salad.

BEEF BOURGUIGNONNE

*This traditional dish can be cooked in half the usual time by
using the combination method.*

SERVES 6

◆

6-8 rashers streaky bacon
225 g/8 oz button onions
1 clove garlic
30 g/1 oz butter
900 g/2 lb lean beef, cubed
115 g/4 oz button mushrooms
30 g/1 oz flour
140 ml/¼ pint red burgundy
1 beef stock cube
150 ml/¼ pint water
Bouquet garni
Salt and pepper
2 tablespoons double cream
1 tablespoon brandy

◆

◀ De-rind the bacon and cut into strips. Peel the
onions and crush the garlic. Melt the butter in a frying pan
and, when sizzling, brown the beef cubes on all sides. Stir
in the bacon, onions and garlic and fry briskly until tinged
gold.

▲▲ Turn into an ovenglass or ceramic casserole and stir
in the mushrooms. Mix the flour and wine together, then
pour over the meat. Cover and cook on Full Power,
stirring occasionally (about 10 minutes) to part cook the
meat. Crumble in the stock cube, add the water and
bouquet garni and season to taste with salt and pepper.

◀ Cover and bake in a preheated 160°C/325°F/Gas
Mark 3 oven until the meat is tender (about 1¼ hours).
Remove the bouquet garni and adjust the seasoning. Stir
in the cream and brandy.

Serve hot with boiled rice.

Note: This dish improves if stored in the refrigerator for 1
day. Reheat, covered, on Full Power, stirring occasionally
(about 6 minutes).

VEAL AND ARTICHOKE CASSEROLE

*Veal is expensive but is more tender than beef. You can
substitute beef if you wish.*

SERVES 4 to 6

◆

40 g/1½ oz flour
½ teaspoon salt
1 teaspoon paprika
2 pinches dried rosemary
½ teaspoon dried basil
¼ teaspoon freshly milled black pepper
900 g/2 lb lean braising veal, cut into 1 cm/½ inch cubes
4 tablespoons salad oil
225 g/8 oz button mushrooms
Garlic salt
140 ml/¼ pint chicken stock
90 ml/3 fl oz medium white wine
1 × 425 g/15 oz can artichoke hearts

◆

◀ Mix the flour, salt, paprika, rosemary, basil and
pepper together. Toss in the veal until well coated. Heat
the oil in a frying pan until hazy, then fry the meat cubes a
few at a time until brown on all sides. Remove with a
slotted spoon, drain and transfer to a microwave-suitable
casserole. Season the mushrooms with garlic salt, add to
the pan and fry briefly. Remove from the pan, drain and
add to the meat.

▲▲ Stir the stock and wine into the casserole, cover and
cook on Full Power until boiling, stirring occasionally
(about 5 minutes). Reduce the setting to Defrost (35%),
cover and continue cooking until the meat is tender (about
30 minutes). Taste and add seasoning if necessary.

Drain the artichokes, slice in half widthways and add to
the meat. Without covering, reheat on Defrost (35%),
stirring occasionally (about 6 minutes).

Serve with freshly boiled egg noodles.

Veal and Artichoke Casserole

BOEUF EN DAUBE

Mushroom and bacon stuffing is wrapped in slices of beef, marinated and cooked with wine and mustard.

SERVES 5 to 6

◆

900 g/2 lb joint topside
8-12 rashers bacon
1 small onion
115 g/4 oz mushrooms
Grated rind of ½ lemon
¼ teaspoon mixed dried herbs
Salt and freshly milled black pepper
1 egg yolk
1 tablespoon fresh white breadcrumbs
140 ml/¼ pint dry red wine
4 cloves garlic
85 g/3 oz butter
140 ml/¼ pint hot water
1 teaspoon French mustard
30 g/1 oz flour

◆

▲▲ Trim the joint and cut into nine slices. Flatten each slice with a cleaver or rolling pin. De-rind the bacon and finely chop. Finely chop the onion. Finely chop the mushrooms.

Put the onion and bacon in a bowl and, without covering, cook on Full Power, stirring occasionally, until the bacon changes colour and the onion is translucent (about 4 minutes). Stir in the mushrooms, lemon rind, herbs and salt and pepper to taste. Mix in the egg and breadcrumbs. Spread a little of the mixture over each beef slice. Roll up and tie with cotton (do not use plastic string).

Put the beef rolls in a dish, pour in the wine and add the garlic cloves. Cover and leave for 12 hours or overnight, turning the rolls over once or twice.

◀ Remove the rolls and drain thoroughly, reserve the marinade but discard the garlic. Heat 55 g/2 oz of the butter in a frying pan and, when hazy, fry the beef rolls briskly on all sides until brown.

▲▲ Put the beef rolls in a flameproof glass casserole and pour over the reserved marinade and hot water. Stir in the mustard, cover and cook on Full Power until the liquid boils (about 7 minutes). Reposition the rolls, cover and cook for a further 5 minutes.

◀ Put the casserole in a preheated 160°C/325°F/Gas Mark 3 oven and bake until the meat is soft (about 45 minutes). Transfer the meat to a hot serving dish and remove the string. Keep warm.

▲▲ Put the remaining butter in a basin and heat on Full Power until melted (about 30 seconds). Stir in the flour, then add 8-10 tablespoons of the hot liquor. Without covering, cook on Full Power, stirring frequently, until the sauce is thick. Pour into the juices in the casserole and, without covering, cook until reheated (about 2 minutes). Taste and add extra seasoning if desired.

Pour over the beef rolls and serve hot with sautéed potatoes and broccoli.

TRADITIONAL ROAST BEEF

The shape of the roast is as important as the cut of beef chosen.

SERVES 8 to 10

◆

1.8 kg/4 lb even-shaped joint beef

◆

▲▲ Put the beef on a ceramic rack in a shallow ovenglass roasting dish. Cover with a slit roasting bag and cook on Full Power until the joint changes colour (about 12 minutes), turning it over after 6 minutes. Spoon away the surplus fat and remove the covering.

◀ Transfer to a preheated 220°C/425°F/Gas Mark 7 oven. Roast until it reaches the required doneness and is brown (30-50 minutes).

CHARING CROSS ROAST

This is an interesting recipe with a novel-shaped meat loaf served with diced vegetables in a brown sauce.

SERVES 6

◆

1 potato
1 carrot
1 small leek
1 tablespoon lemon juice
1 medium onion
680 g/1½ lb lean minced beef
1 thick slice stale bread
½ teaspoon mixed dried herbs
2 tablespoons tomato purée
2 eggs
Salt and freshly milled black pepper
30 g/1 oz butter
2 tablespoons oil
15 g/½ oz flour
1 × 400 g/14 oz can tomato soup
425 ml/¾ pint water

◆

Peel and dice the potato and carrot. Thinly slice the leek. Mix these vegetables with the lemon juice and set aside. Quarter the onion and put in a food processor. Add the minced beef and switch on briefly until mixed. Add the bread, shredded into small pieces, and process again. Add the herbs, tomato purée and eggs and blend to a thick paste. With dampened hands form the mixture into a loaf shape.

◀ Heat the butter and oil in a large frying pan until sizzling. Quickly brown the loaf on all sides. Using two fish slices, lift out and set aside. Stir the flour into the fat in the pan and cook, stirring constantly, until brown. Add the soup and water, blend well, then remove from the heat.

▲▲ Pour the sauce into a large casserole and, without covering, cook on Full Power, stirring frequently, until the sauce thickens slightly (about 6 minutes). Lower the meat loaf into the sauce and spoon some sauce over the top. Drain the vegetables and spoon around the meat. Cover and cook until the meat loaf is cooked through (about 10 minutes) – the sauce will gradually thicken. Remove the meat loaf from the sauce and serve sliced with a generous helping of sauce.

LAMB KHORESH

Sliced tomatoes conceal layers of lamb and aubergine in this Turkish dish.

SERVES 6

◆

1 onion
1 tablespoon oil
900 g/2 lb lean lamb, cubed
1 teaspoon turmeric
2 tablespoons tomato purée
Grated rind and juice of ½ lemon
Salt and freshly milled black pepper
450 g/1 lb aubergines
3 large tomatoes, sliced

◆

▲▲ Without peeling, put the onion in a small bowl and cook on Full Power until soft (about 1½ minutes). Remove the skin and chop the flesh.

◀ Heat the oil in a saucepan over a high heat until hazy. Add the chopped onion and cubes of lamb. Stir briskly until the meat is brown (about 5 minutes). Carefully add water to barely cover (about 450 ml/¾ pint) and add the turmeric, tomato purée, lemon rind and juice. Season to taste. Lower the heat, cover and cook gently until the meat is tender (about 1 hour).

▲▲ Peel and thickly slice the aubergines, put in a large dish and add 4-5 tablespoons of water. Cover and cook on Full Power until tender (about 5 minutes). Drain and season with salt and pepper. Arrange the meat and aubergine in layers in a 1.5 litre/2½ pint dish. Cover with tomato slices and, without covering, cook until hot and the tomato slices are soft (about 3 minutes).

Serve with rice, lentils or mashed potatoes.

MARINADE OF PORK SIENNA

These pork cubes have a hint of juniper and are best served on a bed of rice.

SERVES 4 to 5

◆

680 g/1½ lb pork fillet
1 teaspoon juniper berries
1 clove garlic
2 tablespoons walnut oil
1 tablespoon pine nuts
285 ml/½ pint dry white wine
Grated rind and juice of ½ lemon
Salt and freshly milled black pepper
340 g/12 oz cooked rice

◆

◀ Cut the pork into 1 cm/½ inch cubes and put in a casserole. Crush the juniper berries and add to the pork. Crush and stir in the garlic. Add the oil, pine nuts, wine, lemon rind and juice and season lightly. Cover and leave to stand for 12 hours, stirring occasionally.

Remove the meat and reserve the marinade. Line the grill pan with foil and brown the meat under a fierce heat.
▲▲ Combine the meat and marinade in a microwave-suitable casserole. Cover and cook on Full Power, stirring occasionally, until the meat is just tender (about 10 minutes). Put the rice in a suitable serving dish. Pour over the meat and sauce and, without covering, reheat (about 4 minutes).

GAMMON IN PLUM SAUCE

This recipe is simple but attractive. The gammon steaks are topped with a Victoria plum and served with a plum sauce.

SERVES 6

◆

6 thick slices smoked gammon or ham steaks
Coarsely grated rind and juice of 1 large orange
6 tablespoons plum jelly
3 tablespoons port
1 tablespoon lemon juice
3 ripe Victoria plums
Oil

◆

▲▲ Snip the gammon steaks around the edges and put in a bowl. Just cover with water and, without covering, cook on Full Power until the water boils (about 6 minutes). Drain.

Put the grated rind into a jug, cover with water and bring to the boil (about 1½ minutes). Cook until the water returns to the boil (about 1½ minutes). Drain and rinse well.

Put the jelly in a jug and, without covering, heat until the liquid boils (about 1 minute). Stir in the orange juice, port and lemon juice. Add the orange rind and cook until thickened (about 3 minutes). Stone the plums and arrange the halves on a plate. Cover and cook until tender (about 30 seconds).
◀ Brush the gammon slices with oil and cook on both sides under a hot grill (about 2 minutes each side for thinner steaks, and 4 minutes each side for thicker steaks).
▲▲ Without covering, reheat the sauce on Full Power (about 1½ minutes). Garnish the gammon slices with the plums and pour over the sauce.

Gammon in Plum Sauce and Brandy Snaps (*see page 73*)

ROAST LAMB WITH LIVER AND BACON STUFFING

Although shoulder of lamb is my preferred choice, leg of lamb may be substituted instead if you wish.

SERVES 4 to 6

◆

1 × 1.25 kg/2½ lb joint boned shoulder of lamb
1 medium onion
115 g/4 oz streaky bacon
115 g/4 oz lamb's liver
85 g/3 oz fresh breadcrumbs
½ teaspoon dried sage
Salt and pepper
1 tablespoon cornflour
Gravy browning

◆

▲▲ Trim the fat from the joint. Finely chop the onion. De-rind and chop the bacon. Trim and chop the liver. Put the onion and bacon in a medium bowl and, without covering, cook on Full Power until the bacon is opaque (about 2 minutes). Add the liver. Cover and cook, stirring occasionally, until the liver is just pink (about 2 minutes). Blend in a processor then add the breadcrumbs, sage and salt and pepper to taste. Stuff into the lamb pocket and tie with string.

Put the joint in an ovenglass dish, cover and cook on Full Power until hot (about 10 minutes). Spoon away the excess fat.

◄ Cover the lamb with foil, place in a preheated 190°C/375°F/Gas Mark 5 oven and roast for about 20 minutes. Remove the foil and continue roasting until cooked through and brown (about 25 minutes). Remove the meat and cut off the string. Keep the joint warm.

▲▲ Skim the fat from the dish, measure the juices and make up to 285 ml/½ pint with water. Stir in the cornflour and blend well with the meat juices. Add a few drops of gravy browning and, without covering, cook on Full Power, stirring frequently, until the gravy thickens (about 1 minute). Season with salt and pepper, pour into a gravy boat and serve with the lamb.

LAMB CURRY BRAZILIA

Coriander leaves give this fruity curry its very distinctive flavour.

SERVES 4 to 5

◆

680 g/1½ lb lean lamb
1 clove garlic
2 sticks celery
1 medium onion
4 bay leaves
1 teaspoon whole black peppercorns
2 tablespoons salad oil
About 285 ml/½ pint boiling water
1 tablespoon chopped coriander leaves
Salt
1 green dessert apple
1 tablespoon flour
1 tablespoon curry powder
2 tablespoons grated coconut

◆

Trim, cut up and dice the lamb. Crush the garlic and dice the celery and onion. Tie the bay leaves and peppercorns in a twist of muslin.

◄ Heat the oil in a large heavy-based saucepan until hazy. Toss in the meat and stir briskly to seal. Add boiling water to barely cover. Add the garlic, celery, onion, bag of herbs and coriander leaves, and add salt to taste. Peel core and slice the apple. Stir into the meat. Cover and cook gently until the lamb is tender (about 45 minutes).

Remove the bag of herbs. Strain the stock and make up to 425 ml/¾ pint with cold water. Reserve the vegetables and meat.

▲▲ Mix the flour, curry powder and coconut into the stock. Without covering, cook on Full Power, stirring frequently, until the sauce thickens (about 5 minutes).

Stir the meat and vegetables into the sauce. Season. Cover and reheat, stirring occasionally (about 2 minutes). Preferably serve at once.

To reheat from cold, cover and cook on Full Power (about 5 minutes).

Serve with boiled rice.

PORK TRANCHE

This substantial dish of mashed potatoes and pork is not unlike a Shepherds Pie.

SERVES 6 to 8

◆

1.5 kg/3 lb potatoes
4 spring onions
30 g/1 oz butter
1 egg
Salt and pepper
450 g/1 lb raw minced pork
285 ml/½ pint water
1 chicken stock cube
2 tablespoons dry cider
Pinch of ground cloves
15 g/½ oz flour
4 tablespoons cooked or frozen peas
2 tablespoons flaked almonds
Paprika

◆

◀ Grease a shallow, flameproof ceramic dish. Peel and cut up the potatoes. Finely slice the spring onions and put to one side. Boil the potatoes in salted water. Drain and mash with the butter, egg and salt and pepper to taste.

Meanwhile, put the meat in a bowl, add the water, crumbled stock cube, cider, onions, ground cloves and flour. Season to taste with salt and pepper.

◀◀ Spread half the potatoes in a dish. Cover with meat mixture, spread with peas and top with the remaining potatoes. Without covering, cook on Defrost (35%) until the meat is pale and firm when tested by inserting a round-bladed knife in the centre (about 25 minutes).

◀ Sprinkle with flaked almonds and paprika and brown under a hot grill.

Serve hot with grilled apple rings.

SWEET AND SOUR PORK CHOPS

Pork chops cooked this way are moist and tender. The sultanas are sufficient to sweeten the sauce without recourse to sugar.

SERVES 6

◆

6 pork chops, trimmed
1 clove garlic
1 tablespoon salad oil
40 g/1½ oz flour
425 ml/¾ pint hot chicken stock
2 tablespoons red wine vinegar
1 teaspoon mustard powder
3 drops Tabasco sauce
Salt and pepper
55 g/2 oz sultanas

◆

◀◀ Overlap the chops on a large plate. Without covering, cook on Full Power until the colour lightens (about 8 minutes).

◀ Transfer to a casserole dish. Place in a preheated 180°C/350°F/Gas Mark 4 oven to commence cooking while preparing the sauce.

◀◀ Crush the garlic and combine with the oil in an ovenglass bowl. Stir in the flour. Without covering, cook on Full Power, stirring frequently, until the flour browns (about 3 minutes). Add the stock, vinegar, mustard and Tabasco. Without covering, cook, stirring occasionally, until the sauce thickens (about 4 minutes). Season with salt and pepper and stir in the sultanas.

◀ Pour the sauce over the chops. Cover with the lid and continue baking in the hot oven until the chops are tender (about 40-45 minutes).

Serve with boiled rice.

ROAST PRUNE AND APRICOT STUFFED PORK

My tasters pronounced this delicious. You can substitute sultanas for the prunes if you prefer.

SERVES 4 to 6

◆

1 × 1.8 kg/4 lb joint boneless pork
1 teaspoon mustard powder
85 g/3 oz dried apricots
55 g/2 oz pitted prunes
1 small onion
7 g/¼ oz butter
½ teaspoon dried tarragon
55 g/2 oz fresh breadcrumbs
Grated rind and juice of 1 small lemon
A little beaten egg
Salt and freshly milled black pepper

◆

▲▲ Make a wide incision through the joint from the middle of one cut end towards the other. Rub the outside with mustard powder and make several shallow slashes. Put the apricots and prunes in a basin and just cover with water. Cover the basin and cook on Full Power until tender but not soft (about 5 minutes).

Meanwhile, dice the onion and put in a bowl with the butter and tarragon. Without covering, cook until soft but not brown (about 3 minutes). Mix in the breadcrumbs, lemon rind and juice. Roughly chop the fruit, then add to the onion mixture. Add the egg and stir until blended. Season and press the stuffing into the pork.

Put the joint, stuffing side up, in a glass roasting dish and cook on Full Power for about 8 minutes. Turn the joint over and cook for a further 8 minutes. Spoon away surplus melted fat.

◀ Turn stuffing side up and place the dish in a preheated 200°C/400°F/Gas Mark 6 oven. Pour over the liquid from the fruit, cover with foil and roast for 25 minutes. Remove the foil and continue roasting, basting occasionally, until the crackling is crisp and the centre of the joint is fully cooked (about 25 minutes). Test with a sharp-pointed knife – the juices should run clear.

Transfer the joint to a heated serving dish. Skim off the fat and spoon the juices over the sliced meat.

Roast Prune and Apricot Stuffed Pork and Rhubarb Lattice (*see page 65*)

BACON STUFFED MARROW BAKE

Cook this dish in summer when marrow is in season and at its best. The stuffing can be used in any type of squash or piled onto courgette halves.

SERVES 4 to 6

◆

1 medium onion
115 g/4 oz mushrooms
450 g/1 lb boned bacon (choose a cheap cut)
1 even-shaped marrow (weighing about 1.8 kg/4 lb)
30 g/1 oz butter
55 g/2 oz fresh breadcrumbs
Freshly milled black pepper
30 g/1 oz Parmesan cheese, grated
Sauce
4 tablespoons salad oil
55 g/2 oz flour
570 ml/1 pint milk
¼ teaspoon bay leaf powder
½ teaspoon dried parsley
Pinch of dried thyme
Salt and pepper
85 g/3 oz strong cheese, grated

◆

▲▲ Finely chop the onion and mushrooms. De-rind and mince or finely chop the bacon. Cut the ends off the marrow and peel. Slice the marrow into five or six rings and remove the centre pips.

Put the marrow in a large bowl. Add 6 tablespoons of salted water. Cover and cook on Full Power to slightly soften (about 5 minutes). Leave to stand covered.

Put the butter in a large bowl. Without covering, heat until melted (about 30 seconds). Stir in the onion and cook, stirring occasionally, until soft (about 3 minutes). Add the bacon, cover and continue cooking, stirring frequently, until the colour changes (about 3 minutes). Mix in the mushrooms and cook briefly (about 2 minutes). Drain. Mix in half the breadcrumbs and season with pepper.

Drain and dry the marrow rings. Arrange in a single layer in a casserole dish. Pile the bacon mixture into the rings.

▲▲ To make the sauce, blend the oil, flour and milk in a large bowl. Stir in the bay leaf powder, parsley and thyme. Without covering, cook on Full Power, stirring occasionally, until the sauce thickens (about 5 minutes). Stir

in the strong cheese and season with salt and pepper.

◀ Pour the sauce over the marrow rings. Mix the remaining breadcrumbs with the Parmesan and sprinkle over the sauce. Bake in a preheated 200°C/400°F/Gas Mark 6 oven until golden brown (about 20 minutes).

CROWN OF BACON

This can look fabulous as a centrepiece when serving up a special meal.

SERVES 4 to 6

◆

680 g/1½ lb rolled bacon joint
1 medium onion
115 g/4 oz mushrooms
30 g/1 oz butter
Salt and pepper
Beaten egg for glazing
Pastry
450 g/1 lb plain flour
1 teaspoon salt
170 g/6 oz lard
140 ml/¼ pint milk
2 egg yolks

◆

▲▲ Put the bacon joint in a dish. Cover and part cook on Full Power (about 10 minutes). Drain and leave covered.

Finely chop the onion and thinly slice the mushrooms. Put the onion and butter in a bowl and, without covering, cook, stirring occasionally, until the onion browns (about 5 minutes). Stir in the mushrooms and cook until slightly softened (about 2 minutes). Season with salt and pepper, cover and set aside.

▲▲ To make the pastry, sieve the flour and salt into a warmed bowl. Cut the lard into small pieces and put in a jug with the milk. Without covering, heat on Full Power until steaming but not boiling (about 3 minutes).

Immediately pour into the flour and half mix with a wooden spoon. Beat the egg yolks, add to the bowl and stir vigorously. Leave for a few minutes until cool enough to handle. Knead to a soft but not sticky dough. Roll out three-quarters of the pastry to a circle large enough to wrap around the bacon joint. Cover the remaining pastry with a small upturned bowl.

◀ Spread out the mushroom mixture in the centre of

the pastry circle to the diameter of the bacon. Remove any string and stand the bacon on top of the mushrooms. Lift up the sides of the pastry around and over the bacon and press the edges together. The bacon joint should be completely enclosed. Place seam-side down on a greased baking tray and brush with beaten egg. Roll out the remaining pastry, cutting out three long strips. Use two to cross over the crown and the third to wrap around the base. Roll the trimmings into jewels. Fix to the crown with beaten egg and glaze with remaining egg. Bake in a preheated 230°C/450°F/Gas Mark 8 oven for 15 minutes, then reduce to 160°C/325°F/Gas Mark 3 and leave for about 40 minutes to cook through to the centre.

Slice and serve with green vegetables and grilled tomatoes.

SWEETCORN AND RED PEPPER CHICKEN CASSEROLE

This casserole uses convenience foods and is easy to prepare.

SERVES 6

6 chicken joints, skinned
Salt and pepper
30 g/1 oz flour
30 g/1 oz butter
1 × 314 g/11 oz can sweetcorn
115 g/4 oz frozen peas
1 × 170 g/6 oz can red pimientos
1 × 300 g/10 oz can condensed mushroom soup
140 ml/¼ pint water

Season the chicken joints with salt and pepper and dip in the flour. Heat the butter in a frying pan until sizzling and brown the chicken joints on both sides (about 5 minutes). Stir in the remaining flour.

Transfer to an ovenglass casserole. Stir in the sweetcorn, peas, drained pimientos and soup and season with salt and pepper. Cover and cook on Full Power for 10 minutes, then reposition the chicken and cook for a further 10 minutes. Stir in the water, reposition the chicken again and cook until tender (about 8 minutes). Leave to stand covered for 15 minutes before serving.

HAM, VEAL AND PORK CASSEROLE

This recipe hails from Holland. It is fairly easy and quick to prepare. Any cooked meats may be substituted for the veal and pork, but the ham gives its own characteristic flavour.

SERVES 4

Filling
85 g/3 oz ham
85 g/3 oz roast pork
85 g/3 oz roast beef or veal
1 small onion
115 g/4 oz button mushrooms
30 g/1 oz butter
Topping
450 g/1 lb cooked potatoes
1 tablespoon milk
1 egg, beaten
1 tablespoon freshly chopped parsley
¼ teaspoon grated nutmeg
Salt and freshly milled black pepper
Garnish
30 g/1 oz butter
55 g/2 oz flaked almonds
½ teaspoon hot paprika
1 tablespoon freshly chopped parsley

To prepare the filling, finely chop or mince the meats and mix together. Finely chop the onion and thinly slice the mushrooms. Put the butter in a medium bowl and heat on Full Power until melted (about 1 minute). Stir in the onion and, without covering, cook to soften (about 2 minutes). Add the mushrooms, cover and cook until the juices run freely (about 4 minutes). Layer the vegetables and meat in an ovenproof dish.

To make the topping, put the potatoes in a large bowl. Cover and cook on Full Power until hot (about 2 minutes). Mash the potatoes with the milk and add the egg, parsley and nutmeg. Season to taste with salt and pepper.

Spoon the topping over the meat and vegetables. Dot with butter and sprinkle with almonds, paprika and parsley. Bake in a preheated 190°C/375°F/Gas Mark 5 oven until brown (about 35 minutes).

Serve with seasonal green vegetables.

HAM SOUFFLÉ
WITH PIMIENTO SAUCE

This soufflé is lighter than usual with a slightly piquant sauce which is optional.

SERVES 5 to 6

◆

170 g/6 oz ham
5 eggs
40 g/1½ oz butter
30 g/1 oz flour
200 ml/7 fl oz milk
1 tablespoon bottled fruity sauce
Salt and pepper
Sauce
1 × 170 g/6 oz can pimientos
1 × 227 g/8 oz can tomatoes
1 tablespoon arrowroot
1 teaspoon Worcestershire sauce
Salt and pepper

◆

Grease and flour an 18 cm/7 inch diameter, 1.7 litre/3 pint soufflé dish. Dice the ham and separate the eggs.

▲▲ Put the butter in a medium bowl and, without covering, heat on Full Power until melted (about 1 minute). Stir in the flour and cook until the roux seems to be drying (about 20 seconds). Add the milk and cook, stirring frequently with a wire whisk, until the sauce thickens (about 2 minutes). Stir in the fruity sauce and season with salt and pepper. Beat and strain in the egg yolks. Mix in the ham.

◀ Using beaters, whip the egg whites to stiff peaks. Stir a little into the sauce, then fold in the rest with a metal spoon. Pour the mixture into the prepared dish and bake in a preheated 200°C/400°F/Gas Mark 6 oven until puffed up and golden brown (about 40 minutes).

▲▲ Meanwhile, prepare the pimiento sauce. Liquidize the drained pimientos and tomatoes (with their juice). Pour into a medium bowl, stir in the arrowroot and Worcestershire sauce and add salt and pepper to taste. Without covering, cook on Full Power, stirring frequently, until the sauce thickens (about 4 minutes).

Serve the soufflé immediately with a little sauce spooned over.

Ham Soufflé with Pimiento Sauce

ROAST CHICKEN BOURSIN

The garlic and herb cheese imparts a splendid flavour to an otherwise ordinary roast chicken.

SERVES 4 to 6

◆

1.5 kg/3½ lb oven-ready chicken with giblets
¼ onion
3 slices carrot
1 clove garlic
1 × 100 g/3½ oz packet garlic and herb full-cream cheese
55 g/2 oz fresh white breadcrumbs
15 g/½ oz butter
2 tablespoons flour
Salt and freshly milled black pepper

◆

▲▲ Trim the chicken wings and leg tips. Discard the gizzard. Rinse the giblets and cut in half or slash. Put the tips and giblets in a large bowl and add 450 ml/¾ pint of water, the onion, carrot and peeled garlic clove. Part cover and cook on Full Power until boiling (about 4 minutes). Skim, then part cover again and continue cooking to obtain a well-flavoured stock (about 30 minutes). Strain and set aside.

Dry the inside of the chicken with kitchen paper. Blend the cheese and breadcrumbs together and stuff into the neck end. Put the chicken in an ovenglass roasting dish and dot with butter. Without covering, cook on Full Power for 10 minutes.

◀ Transfer to a preheated 200°C/400°F/Gas Mark 6 oven and roast until tender. Remove the chicken to a hot serving dish.

▲▲ Skim the fat from the juices in the dish, stir in the flour and add 285 ml/½ pint of giblet stock. Season with salt and pepper. Using oven gloves, put the dish in the microwave and without covering, cook on Full Power, stirring frequently, until the gravy thickens. Adjust seasoning and pour into a gravy boat.

Serve the chicken sliced with traditional roast potatoes and cabbage, and hand the gravy separately.

CHICKABURGERS

These burgers are lightly fried and can be served at any meal with most accompaniments.

SERVES 4 to 8

◆

1 medium onion
340 g/12 oz cooked chicken meat, skinned and boned
30 g/1 oz butter
30 g/1 oz flour
½ chicken stock cube
140 ml/¼ pint hot water
2 tablespoons lemon juice
2 tablespoons freshly chopped parsley
½ teaspoon turmeric
Salt and freshly milled black pepper
2 eggs
5-6 tablespoons breadcrumbs or matzo meal
5-6 tablespoons oil for frying

◆

▲▲ Finely chop the onion. Very finely chop the chicken meat by hand or in a food processor.

Put the butter in a large bowl and, without covering, heat on Full Power until melted (about 45 seconds). Stir in the onion and cook, stirring occasionally, until soft (about 4 minutes). Stir in the flour and cook until puffy (about 45 seconds). Crumble in the stock cube and add the hot water. Without covering, cook, stirring occasionally with a wire whisk, until the sauce is very thick (about 1 minute). Thin down with lemon juice and mix in the parsley and turmeric. Add the chicken. Season with salt and pepper and bind with 1 lightly beaten egg. Leave until cold.

◀ Divide the mixture and shape into eight burgers. Dip in the remaining egg, beaten, then coat with breadcrumbs, pressing them well in. Pour 3-4 tablespoons of oil into a frying pan and heat until hazy. Fry the burgers for 2-3 minutes on each side, adding more oil if needed. Drain on kitchen paper.

Serve with sliced tomato and cucumber.

CHICKEN AND HAM PIE

Take time to decorate this and glaze thickly with beaten egg and your pie will look and taste like a masterpiece.

SERVES 4 to 6

115 g/4 oz ham
680 g/1½ lb cooked chicken
1 medium onion
115 g/4 oz streaky bacon
225 g/8 oz ready-to-roll puff pastry
30 g/1 oz flour
285 ml/½ pint hot water
1 chicken stock cube
1 teaspoon tomato ketchup
Salt and pepper
Beaten egg for glazing

Dice the ham and cut up the chicken into bite-sized pieces. Finely chop the onion. De-rind and chop the bacon. Roll out the pastry to fit the top of an oval 850 ml/1½ pint pie dish. Leave the pastry in a cool place.

▲▲ Put the onion and bacon in a basin and, without covering, cook on Full Power, stirring occasionally, until soft (about 4 minutes). Stir in the flour and continue cooking, stirring frequently, until the flour browns (about 2 minutes). Add the hot water and the crumbled stock cube. Cook, stirring frequently with a wooden spoon, until the sauce thickens (about 3 minutes). Stir in the tomato ketchup, ham and chicken and season sparingly with salt and pepper.

◀ Pour into the pie dish. Damp the edges of the dish and fix on the pastry lid, being careful not to stretch it. Knock up the edges with a table knife and brush the top only with the egg glaze. Bake in a preheated 220°C/425°F/Gas Mark 7 oven until the pastry is risen and golden brown (about 35 minutes).

CHICKEN PAPRIKASH

Chicken pieces are cooked in a rich, deep red Hungarian sauce.

SERVES 5

1 × 1.5 kg/3½ lb chicken, jointed, or
1.5 kg/3½ lb chicken joints
2 large onions
Salt and pepper
85 g/3 oz flour
55 g/2 oz butter
2 tablespoons salad oil
1 tablespoon sweet paprika
4 tablespoons tomato purée
425 ml/¾ pint water
115 g/4 oz ready-to-roll puff pastry
Oil for frying

▲▲ Skin the chicken. Finely slice the onions and put to one side. Put the chicken pieces in a casserole and season with salt and pepper on both sides. Cover and cook on Full Power, repositioning twice, until the chicken is opaque (about 15 minutes).

◀ Remove the chicken pieces from the casserole and dip in the flour. Heat the butter and oil in a frying pan until hazy. Quickly brown the chicken pieces a few at a time.

▲▲ Meanwhile, put the onion slices in the casserole. Cover and cook on Full Power until slightly softened (about 5 minutes). Stir in the paprika, tomato purée and water and, without covering, cook until boiling (about 3 minutes). Stir vigorously, then season with salt and pepper.

◀ Place the chicken pieces in the sauce, cover the casserole and transfer to a preheated 180°C/350°F/Gas Mark 4 oven and cook until tender (about 30 minutes).

Meanwhile, roll out the pastry and, using a 5 cm/2 inch round cutter, cut out crescent shapes by moving the cutter down the length of the pastry at 2.5 cm/1 inch intervals. Alternatively, cut out leaf shapes using a leaf cutter. Chill in the freezer for 10 minutes.

Fry the pastry shapes both sides in 2.5 cm/1 inch of hot oil. Drain well and serve each portion of chicken garnished with pastry shapes.

Saté Ayam

SATÉ AYAM

This attractive skewered chicken is served with a peanut sauce.

SERVES 8 to 10

◆

8-10 chicken breasts, skinned and boned
4 cloves garlic
4 tablespoons soy sauce
2 tablespoons soft brown sugar
4 tablespoons lemon juice
Sauce
55 g/2 oz desiccated coconut
285 ml/½ pint water
1 tablespoon walnut oil
1 bunch spring onions
30 g/1 oz chopped cashew nuts
¼ teaspoon chilli compound powder
1 teaspoon soft brown sugar
8 tablespoons crunchy peanut butter
1 tablespoon soy sauce
1 tablespoon lemon juice
225-350 g/8-12 oz cooked long-grain rice

◆

Prick the chicken deeply. Cut into bite-sized pieces. Crush the garlic and put in a large bowl with the soy sauce, sugar and lemon juice. Mix in the chicken, cover and leave in a cool place for 2 hours. Stir occasionally.

▲▲ To make the sauce, stir the coconut into the water in a jug or bowl and cook, without covering, on Full Power until boiling (about 1½ minutes). Stir, cover and set aside for 30 minutes.

Put the oil in a bowl, finely slice the spring onions and stir into the oil. Cover and cook until soft. Mix in the cashew nuts, chilli compound powder, sugar and peanut butter. Without covering, heat, stirring frequently for about 1 minute. Strain in the coconut liquid. Without covering, cook, stirring occasionally until thickened (about 3 minutes), then mix in the soy sauce and lemon juice.

◄ Remove the chicken from the marinade and thread onto skewers. Cook under a hot grill or on a barbecue, turning the skewers so that all surfaces are browned and the chicken is properly cooked (about 10 minutes). Baste with the marinade during cooking.

▲▲ Reheat the sauce on Full Power (about 1 minute). Put the rice in a dish and reheat (about 2 minutes).

Serve the skewered chicken on top of the rice and pour over the sauce. For a special meal, garnish with a tomato rose, lime slices, purple sage and chopped chives.

POULET ROSÉ DU PAYS

In this casserole, chicken and finely sliced mushrooms are cooked in a deliciously pink, glowing sauce. The shade will deepen during a prolonged standing time due to the colour being released by the beetroot.

SERVES 5 to 6

◆

680 g/1½ lb skinned and boned raw chicken
225 g/8 oz button mushrooms
1 large red pepper
30 to 45 g/1 to 1½ oz cooked beetroot
70 g/2½ oz flour
2 teaspoons cornflour
Salt and freshly milled black pepper
1 tablespoon salad oil
40 g/1½ oz butter
285 ml/½ pint rose wine
285 ml/½ pint hot chicken stock or water and stock cube

◆

Cut the chicken into bite-sized pieces. Thinly slice the mushrooms. Core, deseed and cut the red pepper in strips. Peel and dice the beetroot.

▲▲ Put the mushrooms and peppers in a large suitable casserole. Cover and cook on Full Power until the juices flow and the peppers are softening (about 5 minutes).

Meanwhile, combine the flour and cornflour and season generously with salt and pepper. Use a little of the mixture to lightly dust the chicken pieces.

◄ Put the oil and butter in a large frying pan and heat until foaming, then briskly fry the chicken until they are just golden.

Blend the remaining seasoned flours with the wine and stir into the mushrooms and peppers. Add the beetroot, stock, and then the chicken pieces.

▲▲ Cover and cook on Full Power, stirring occasionally, until the chicken and mushrooms are tender and the sauce has thickened (about 10 minutes). Adjust the seasoning and serve from the casserole with spaghetti or boiled rice.

POTATO BASKET

As the name suggests this is a basket made from mashed potatoes filled with minced beef and vegetables.

SERVES 6

◆

1.5 kg/3 lb potatoes
Salt and pepper
30 g/1 oz butter
2 eggs, beaten
1 leek
2 frankfurters
1 small green pepper
225 g/8 oz lean minced beef
55 g/2 oz sweetcorn
55 g/2 oz frozen peas
1 teaspoon cornflour
4 tablespoons red wine
Celery salt
Garlic powder

◆

◀ Peel the potatoes. Cut up and cook in a saucepan in boiling salted water until soft (about 25 minutes). Drain, mash, then press through a sieve. Season and beat in the butter, then beat in three-quarters of the egg. Put the mixture into a piping bag fitted with a 1 cm/½ inch plain nozzle. Grease a 20 cm/8 inch ovenglass serving dish and pipe half the potato over the base. Pipe the remainder of the potato around the border, gradually building it up to a solid wall, and brush with the remaining egg.

Bake in a preheated 180°C/350°F/Gas Mark 4 oven until brown (about 25 minutes).

▲▲ Meanwhile, slice the leek and frankfurters. Core, de-seed and dice the pepper. Put the beef in a bowl and, without covering, cook on Full Power, stirring occasionally, until the colour changes and the fat oozes (about 4 minutes). Drain away the surplus fat.

Put the sliced leek in a bowl, add 4 tablespoons of salted water and cover and cook until tender (about 2 minutes). Add the sweetcorn, peas and diced pepper. Cover and cook until tender (about 2 minutes). Drain. Mix the beef with the vegetables. Stir in the frankfurters and season sparingly with salt and generously with pepper. Cover and cook until hot (about 3 minutes).

Blend the cornflour with the meat juices and wine in a bowl and, without covering, cook, stirring frequently, until thickened (about 2 minutes). Season with celery salt and garlic powder, then mix into the meat and vegetables. Fill the potato basket with the mixture and serve hot.

ROAST PARSNIPS

These are a natural companion for the Sunday roast. Choose young moist parsnips for best results.

SERVES 4

◆

680 g/1½ lb parsnips
Salt
4 tablespoons vegetable oil

◆

▲▲ Peel the parsnips and remove the tops and tips. Cut into quarters lengthwise and remove the hard core, then cut into 5 cm/2 inch lengths and put into a casserole. Add sufficient salted water to reach halfway up the parsnips. Cover with the lid and cook on Full Power until tender but not soft (about 8 minutes). Drain thoroughly and pat dry with kitchen paper.

◀ Put the oil in a shallow roasting dish and heat in a preheated 200°C/400°F/Gas Mark 6 oven until hot (about 5 minutes). Stir in the parsnips and roast, basting occasionally, until nicely browned (about 45 minutes). The parsnips may be roasted around the joint if preferred.

ROAST POTATOES

These are a real time saver.

SERVES 4 to 5

◆

900 g/2 lb potatoes
Salt
1 tablespoon flour
4 tablespoons vegetable oil

◆

▲▲ Peel and cut up the potatoes. Put in a casserole and add 140 ml/¼ pint water. Cover and cook on Full Power, stirring occasionally, until the potatoes are just resistant when a fork is inserted (about 12 minutes). Drain thoroughly, season with salt and toss in the flour.

◀ Put the oil in a large roasting tin and put into a preheated 220°C/425°F/Gas Mark 7 oven for about 5 minutes. Carefully put in the potatoes, preferably in a single layer, and, without covering, bake, turning the potatoes over once, until crisp and golden (about 30 minutes).

PIROSHKIS

Piroshkis resemble small Scotch eggs, and are balls of minced meat wrapped in a potato casing.

SERVES 6 to 8

◆

4 × 225 g/8 oz baking potatoes
1 medium onion
1 egg
3 tablespoons flour
1 teaspoon baking powder
Salt and pepper
1 tablespoon salad oil
225 g/8 oz leftover roast beef
2 hard-boiled eggs
Oil for deep-frying

◆

▲▲ Scrub and prick the potatoes well. Chop the onion. Put the potatoes in the microwave and cook on Full Power until soft (about 16 minutes). Halve and scoop out the pulp. Discard the skins. Mix the raw egg, flour and baking powder with the mashed potatoes and season well.

Put the onion and 1 tablespoon of oil in a medium bowl and, without covering, cook, stirring occasionally, until soft but not coloured (about 2 minutes). Mince the meat, hard-boiled eggs and onion together and season to taste. Shape into eight or twelve balls, then chill until firm.

Divide the potato mixture into a similar number of pieces, form into balls, then flatten into circles. Place one meat ball in the centre of each potato circle, and mould the potato around to completely enclose the meat. Chill to stiffen slightly.

◀ Fill a deep pan one-third full with oil. Heat to 190°C/375°F and deep-fry the Piroshkis until golden. Drain on kitchen paper and serve with mayonnaise or horseradish sauce.

ROAST STUFFED ONIONS

Serve as a filling family meal, or dress up with an Espagnole sauce and the recipe then becomes suitable for entertaining.

SERVES 6

6 medium onions
25 g/1 oz butter
Generous shake of Worcestershire sauce
55 g/2 oz cooked rice
55 g/2 oz grated cheese
170 g/6 oz minced cooked lamb
Salt and freshly milled black pepper
6 rashers streaky bacon
1 frankfurter

▲▲ Skin the onions and put whole in a shallow dish. Cover and cook on Full Power until tender but not soft (about 6 minutes). Remove with a slotted spoon and leave to cool. Remove a sliver from the top of each onion and scoop out the centre with a spoon or grapefruit knife, leaving a firm wall. Chop the centres finely. Set aside half for use in another recipe.

Put the butter in a bowl and heat until melted (about 1 minute). Stir in the Worcestershire sauce, chopped onion, rice, cheese and lamb. Season with salt and pepper.

◀ Stuff the lamb mixture into the onions. Wrap each onion loosely in greased foil, drawing up and twisting the edges dolly-bag fashion. Bake in a preheated 200°C/400°F/Gas Mark 6 oven for 30 minutes.

▲▲ Meanwhile de-rind the bacon and stretch the rashers with the back of a table knife. Roll up the rashers and place on a plate lined with kitchen paper. Cover with kitchen paper. Cook on Full Power until the bacon is ready (about 2 minutes), then remove from the kitchen paper. Slice the frankfurter into six, put on kitchen paper and heat for 30 seconds.

Unwrap the onions, top each with a bacon roll and frankfurter slice and secure with a cocktail stick. Serve the onions on a bed of freshly cooked, shredded cabbage.

COURGETTE FRITTERS

This is a more-ish way of serving courgettes – no eggs are necessary for the batter.

SERVES 6

◆

680 g/1½ lb firm courgettes
Freshly milled black pepper
½ teaspoon grated nutmeg
170 g/6 oz Besan flour
Salt
About 140 ml/¼ pint water
Fresh oil for deep-frying
2 tablespoons freshly chopped parsley

◆

▲▲ Trim the courgettes. Halve lengthwise, then cut into 2.5 cm/1 inch chunks. Put into a bowl and season with pepper and nutmeg. Stir, cover and cook on Full Power stirring once, until slightly tender (about 5 minutes). Drain.

◄ Make a thick batter with the Besan flour and water. Season with salt and mix in the courgettes.

Heat the oil to 185°C/360°F and deep-fry the courgette chunks a few at a time until golden. Drain on kitchen paper. Sprinkle with chopped parsley and serve hot.

Chicken Paprikash (*see page 49*), Courgette Fritters and Roast Potatoes

VEGETABLE GRATIN

Potatoes and cabbage make up this most economical dish.

SERVES 4 to 5

◆

450 g/1 lb potatoes
1 teaspoon stock granules
2 large onions
30 g/1 oz butter or margarine
450 g/1 lb Savoy cabbage
1 tablespoon freshly chopped parsley
1 teaspoon dried thyme
1 teaspoon carraway seeds (optional)
Salt and freshly milled black pepper
115 g/4 oz Cheddar cheese, grated

◆

▲▲ Peel the potatoes and cut into 5 mm/¼ inch slices. Put 6 tablespoons of water in a casserole and sprinkle with stock granules. Spread out the potatoes in the casserole, cover and cook on Full Power until the slices can be pierced with a knife but are not soft enough to mash (about 5 minutes). Leave covered while cooking the onions and cabbage.

Thinly slice the onions and place with the butter in a large bowl. Cover and cook, stirring occasionally, until soft but not brown (about 10 minutes). Thinly shred the cabbage. Mix into the onions, adding the parsley, thyme and carraway seeds. Season with plenty of black pepper. Cover and cook, stirring occasionally, until the cabbage is nearly cooked (about 5 minutes).

◀ Drain the potatoes if necessary. Carefully remove the top layer. Season with salt. Butter the inside of the dish above the layers of potato. Arrange the cabbage mixture over the potatoes, season with salt and top with the remaining potato slices. Sprinkle with the cheese. Bake at 220°C/425°F/Gas Mark 7 until brown (about 30 minutes). Serve hot.
Note: If necessary, this can be reheated, uncovered, in the microwave (about 4 minutes).

MUSHROOM FILLED PEPPERS

Stuffed peppers can sometimes be too filling because of their substantial filling. These contain a light, creamy mushroom sauce and are finished with grated cheese.

SERVES 4

◆

4 large green peppers
450 g/1 lb button mushrooms
1 small onion
30 g/1 oz butter
35 g/1¼ oz flour
2 tablespoons cold milk
285 ml/½ pint single cream
Salt and freshly milled black pepper
55 g/2 oz Cheddar cheese, grated

◆

▲▲ Cut off and discard the lids which are cut from the stalk end of the peppers. De-seed, rinse and shake out excess moisture. Quarter the mushrooms. Chop the onion. Put the peppers, cut side down, in a shallow ovenglass dish and, without covering, cook on Full power until blanched (about 2 minutes). Drain and set aside.

Put the butter in a bowl and heat until melted (about 1 minute). Stir in the onion and, without covering, cook until slightly soft (about 1½ minutes). Add the mushrooms, cover and cook, stirring occasionally, until the juices flow (about 6 minutes).

Mix the flour with the cold milk and stir into the mixture. Blend in the cream. Without covering, cook, stirring occasionally, until the sauce thickens (about 3 minutes). Season with salt and pepper.

◀ Turn the peppers so the open ends are upwards and fill with the mushrooms and sauce. Sprinkle the tops with grated cheese. Bake, uncovered, in a preheated 200°C/400°F/Gas Mark 6 oven until golden on top (about 20 minutes).

CARROT NUT ROAST

This nutritious meal could also be served sliced and garnished with salad as a starter. It is best when served with a rich brown sauce.

SERVES 6-7

◆

1 medium onion
1 medium carrot
3 ripe tomatoes
30 g/1 oz butter
225 g/8 oz chopped mixed nuts
1 tablespoon flour
½ teaspoon dried thyme
½ teaspoon dried dill weed
2 eggs
½ teaspoon yeast extract
½ vegetable stock cube
Salt and freshly milled black pepper

◆

▲▲ Quarter the onion. Slice the carrot. Quarter the tomatoes. Mix together in a large bowl and add the butter. Cover and cook on Full Power, stirring occasionally, until the vegetables are tender (about 5 minutes).

Spread the nuts on greaseproof or non-stick baking parchment and, without covering, cook, stirring frequently until beginning to brown (about 2½ minutes). Tip into a food processor and blend until pulverized. Add the flour, thyme and dill weed. Process briefly then blend in the eggs, yeast extract and crumbled stock cube. Season sparingly with salt and generously with black pepper. Mix in the vegetables and process briefly, if liked.

◄ Grease a 450 g/1 1lb loaf tin and line the base and ends with a strip of non-stick baking parchment. Spoon in the mixture, press down lightly and smooth the top. Bake in a preheated 190°C/375°F/Gas Mark 5 oven until brown (about 35 minutes). Loosen the sides, remove the roast carefully from the tin.

Serve hot with the brown sauce (opposite) and green vegetables.

RICH BROWN SAUCE

This sauce is easy to prepare and freezes well. It is a perfect accompaniment to the Carrot Nut Roast, and can be served with any roast meat.

◆

30 g/1 oz flour
1 tablespoon vegetable oil
1 medium onion
140 ml/¼ pint red wine
1 tablespoon tomato purée
1 dark beef stock cube
115 g/4 oz flat mushrooms, finely chopped
1 rasher rindless back bacon
450 ml/¾ pint hot water
Salt and freshly milled black pepper
¼ teaspoon bay leaf powder

◆

▲▲ Put the flour in a 1 litre/1¾ pint ovenglass bowl. Without covering, cook on Full Power, stirring every minute, until the flour is beige. (The bowl will become very hot, so oven gloves are advisable.) Stir in the oil, followed by all the remaining ingredients. Cook, un-covered, stirring occasionally, until the vegetables and bacon are soft (about 10 minutes). Purée in the liquidizer and reheat before serving.

ANCHOVY AND OLIVE PIZZA

Use a large baking tray as the pizza tends to spread considerably during cooking.

SERVES 4 to 6

❖

225 g/8 oz plain flour
½ teaspoon salt
30 g/1 oz butter
About 140 ml/¼ pint water
¼ teaspoon caster sugar
1 tablespoon dried yeast
Topping
1 small onion
1 tablespoon salad oil
1 × 400 g/14 oz can chopped tomatoes
1 teaspoon dried oregano
Salt and freshly milled black pepper
1 × 50 g/2 oz can anchovy fillets
85 g/3 oz Mozzarella cheese, thinly sliced
8-12 pitted black olives, halved
30 g/1 oz Cheddar cheese, grated

❖

▲▲ To make the base, sift the flour and salt into a mixing bowl. Rub in the butter. Heat the water in a jug on Full Power until warm to the touch (about 30 seconds). Stir in the sugar and, when dissolved, sprinkle with the yeast and whisk with a fork. Leave in a warm place until frothy.

Make a hollow in the flour, add the yeast liquid and knead until no longer sticky. Cover with cling film and leave in a warm place until doubled in size. If microwave space is available, uncover and boost the dough for 10 seconds every 10 minutes.

▲▲ Finely slice the onion. Put in a large bowl with the oil, cover and cook on Full Power until the onion is soft (about 3 minutes). Stir in the tomatoes and oregano and, without covering, cook, stirring occasionally, until thickened (about 8 minutes). Season sparingly.

◀ Drain the anchovy fillets and halve lengthwise. Press out the dough on a greased baking tray to about 20 cm/8 inch in diameter. Spread over the tomato topping and cover with Mozzarella. Arrange the anchovies and olives and sprinkle with the Cheddar cheese. Leave in a warm place for 10 minutes.

Bake in a preheated 200°C/400°F/Gas Mark 6 oven until the pizza base is crisp (about 25 minutes).

SPINACH AND RICOTTA SLICE

Serve in small portions as a starter or with tomato salad as a main course. Although the dish will keep for a day or two, the colour will gradually fade.

SERVES 6 to 8

❖

Crumble base
85 g/3 oz plain wholewheat flour
85 g/3 oz plain white flour
Pinch salt
85 g/3 oz hard margarine
1 tablespoon sesame seeds
Filling
225 g/8 oz cottage cheese
225 g/8 oz ricotta cheese
5 tablespoons concentrated tomato paste
225 g/8 oz freshly cooked chopped spinach
1 tablespoon gelatine powder
Salt and freshly milled black pepper
To garnish:
Sesame seeds and finely chopped chives

❖

◀ To make the crumble base, mix the flours and salt together. Add the margarine, cut up with a knife, then rub in with the fingertips to a texture resembling fine crumbs. Mix in the sesame seeds. Press the crumble mixture into the base of a 20 cm/8 inch square ovenproof dish and bake in a pre-heated oven 200°C/400°F/Gas mark 6 until cooked and golden (about 20 minutes). Leave to cool, then chill in the tin.

▲▲ To make the filling, beat the cheeses and tomato paste together, preferably using a food processor. Drain the spinach, reserving the juice. Stir 3 tablespoons of the spinach juice or water, and the gelatine in a jug and, without covering, heat on Full Power until steaming (about 45 seconds). Stir until dissolved. Beat the spinach into the cheese and continue beating while pouring in the dissolved gelatine from a height. Season to taste with salt and pepper.

Spoon into the crumble base and leave in a cool place – not the freezer – until set.

Garnish with lines of sesame seeds and chopped chives. Slice and serve cold from the dish.

Anchovy and Olive Pizza

WHEATMEAL LENTIL PIE

This is an enchanting, rich brown wholemeal pastry which encases a deliciously firm filling.

SERVES 4-5

◆

Filling
1 medium onion
15 g/½ oz margarine
170 g/6 oz red lentils
115 g/4 oz red Leicester cheese, grated
1 tablespoon freshly chopped parsley
2 hard-boiled eggs
Salt and pepper
Pastry
140 g/5 oz hard margarine
285 g/10 oz wholemeal plain flour
1 egg
3 tablespoons water
2 tablespoons milk
¼ teaspoon salt
Milk for brushing

◆

▲▲   To make the filling, finely chop the onion. Put the margarine in a large bowl and, without covering, heat on Full Power until melted (about 20 seconds). Stir in the onion and continue cooking until soft (about 3 minutes).

Put the lentils in a sieve and wash under hot running water. Stir into the onion and cook, stirring occasionally, for about 5 minutes. Add boiling water to reach about 5 cm/2 inches above the level of the lentils (about 425 ml/¾ pint). Partly cover and cook, stirring occasionally, until soft (about 20 minutes). Drain if necessary. Mix in the cheese and parsley. Chop and add the eggs. Cover and set aside while making the pastry.

To make the pastry, rub the margarine into the flour. Beat the egg, water, milk and salt together. Sprinkle over the pastry crumbs and stir to a manageable dough. Add another tablespoon of water if needed. Knead lightly and roll out half the pastry on a floured surface. Use to line 20 cm/8 inch round pie dish. Fill with the lentil mixture. Roll out the remaining pastry to form a lid, dampening the edges and crimping to seal. Use any pastry scraps to make leaves. Brush with milk. Chill for 30 minutes.

▲▲   Preheat the oven to 200°C/400°F/Gas Mark 6 and bake the pie for 20 minutes. Reduce the temperature to 190°C/375°F/Gas Mark 5 and continue cooking for a further 20-35 minutes until the pastry underneath is completely cooked.

CHEESE AND CHIVE PIE

This is a simple supper dish to be served on its own or, if preferred, with green vegetables or a salad.

SERVES 4 to 5

◆

450 g/1 lb potatoes
Small knob of butter
6 tablespoons milk
Salt and pepper
3 eggs
150 g/5 oz Cheddar cheese, grated
2 tablespoons chopped chives
1 tablespoon freshly chopped parsley

◆

◀   Peel the potatoes and cut into chunks. Cook in boiling salted water until soft (about 20 minutes). Drain and mash with butter and 2 tablespoons of milk. Season with salt and pepper to taste.

▲▲   Grease a 1.2 litre/2 pint flameproof ceramic pie dish. Separate the eggs and beat the yolks with the rest of the milk. Mix in the potatoes, cheese, chives and parsley. Season to taste. Beat the egg whites to soft peaks. Fold into the potato mixture. Spoon into the pie dish.

Without covering, cook on Full Power until the cheese has melted and the mixture is hot all the way through (about 3 minutes).

◀   Brown under the grill (about 5 minutes).

PICNIC PIE

*This looks like a traditional pork pie, but tastes
so much better.*

SERVES 6

❖

225 g/8 oz rashers bacon
1 onion
170 g/6 oz mushrooms
30 g/1 oz flour
140 ml/¼ pint milk
Freshly milled black pepper
170 g/6 oz sausages
450 g/1 lb puff pastry
115 g/4 oz Edam cheese, grated
2 hard-boiled eggs, finely chopped
Beaten egg for glazing

❖

▲▲   Remove the rind and slice the bacon into thin strips. Finely chop the onion and slice the mushrooms. Mix the bacon and onion in a large bowl. Without covering, cook on Full Power, stirring occasionally, until the bacon is cooked (about 3 minutes). Stir in the mushrooms and, without covering, cook until soft (about 2 minutes). Stir in the flour, then add the milk. Without covering, cook until thick, stirring occasionally (about 5 minutes). Season with pepper and set aside.

Separate the sausages. Place in the microwave between two sheets of kitchen paper. Part cook until the colour changes (about 1½ minutes), repositioning the sausages after 1 minute. Do not overcook.

◀   Line an oblong 1.25 litre/2¼ pint loaf tin with foil, folding the edges out over the rim. Roll the pastry to a rectangle 3 mm/⅛ inch thick. Cut off a section to form the lid, using the remainder of the pastry to line the loaf dish. Save the trimmings to make pastry leaves.

Slice the sausages thickly and arrange in the base of the dish. Cover with cheese, then sprinkle with chopped egg. Cover with the bacon mixture. Dampen the edges of the pastry, place the lid over the filling and crimp the edges. Glaze with beaten egg. Decorate with glazed pastry leaves.

Bake in the centre of a preheated 200°C/400°F/Gas Mark 6 until golden brown on top (about 35 minutes). Leave to cool. Lift the pie out with the edges of the foil. Serve in slices.

LEEK AND ONION TART

*This tart is really pretty with its variegated green colours.
It has a soft texture and is ideal for parties.*

SERVES 4

❖

225 g/8 oz ready-to-roll shortcrust pastry
680 g/1½ lb leeks
1 large onion
55 g/2 oz butter
1 tablespoon freshly chopped parsley
Salt and pepper
4 tablespoons milk
2 eggs

❖

◀   Roll out the pastry on a floured board and fit into a 20 cm/8 inch greased round pie dish. Cover with foil, pressing it close to the pastry. Bake blind in a preheated 200°C/400°F/Gas Mark 6 oven for 15 minutes. Remove the foil and bake for a further 5 minutes. Remove the flan from the oven and reduce the oven temperature to 180°C/350°F/Gas Mark 4.

▲▲   While the pastry is baking, chop the white part of the leeks and chop the onion. Put the butter in a large bowl and, without covering, heat on Full Power until melted (about 1½ minutes). Stir in the onion and leeks, cover and cook, stirring occasionally, until soft (about 10 minutes). Add the parsley and season with salt and pepper.

Put the milk in a jug and, without covering, heat for about 30 seconds. Beat the eggs, then beat into the milk. Stir into the leeks and onions. Adjust the seasoning.

◀   Pour into the pastry case and bake at 180°C/350°F/Gas Mark 4 to complete setting (about 15 minutes). Serve hot or cold.

SAVOURY BLINTZES

These square pancake parcels have a creamy filling with a hint of cheese.

SERVES 6 to 8

◈

Pancakes
2 eggs
230 ml/8 fl oz milk
140 g/5 oz plain flour
1 tablespoon salad oil
Filling
1 large onion
15 g/½ oz butter
450 g/1 lb cottage cheese
1 egg
3 tablespoons soured cream
Salt and pepper
30 g/1 oz butter for brushing

◈

◁ To make the pancakes, beat the eggs until frothy. Stir in the milk, gradually work in the flour and stir to a smooth batter. Stir in the oil. Cover and set aside for 1 hour.

Stir thoroughly but do not beat. Heat a well-greased non-stick 18 cm/7 inch frying pan. Using 2-3 tablespoons of batter for each, make nine thick pancakes, cooking them on one side only. Stack interleaved with greaseproof paper or cling film.

▲▲ To make the filling, finely chop the onion and put in a bowl with the butter. Cover and cook on Full Power, stirring occasionally, until the onion is soft and beginning to brown (about 7 minutes). Purée in a liquidizer with the cheese, egg and soured cream. Season with salt and pepper. Place a generous spoonful of the filling on the centre of the cooked side of each pancake. Form into packets – fold up one edge, then fold in the sides and fold over the remaining edge.

Put the butter in a small bowl and, without covering, heat until melted (about 30 seconds). Brush a little of the butter on a baking tray. Arrange the pancake parcels on the tray. Pour the remaining butter over them.

◁ Bake in a preheated 200°C/400°F/Gas Mark 6 oven until the Blintzes are crisp and brown.

Serve with a cooked green bean salad, dressed with vinaigrette.

GOLDEN EGG BALLS

Serve as a vegetarian meal with mayonnaise, or as a garnish with casseroled chicken for non-vegetarians as a starter.

MAKES 12

◈

4 hard-boiled eggs
55 g/2 oz butter
55 g/2 oz flour
285 ml/½ pint milk
Salt and pepper
¼ teaspoon mustard powder
1 tablespoon chopped mixed nuts
1 tablespoon freshly chopped parsley
1 egg, beaten
55 g/2 oz fresh breadcrumbs
Oil for deep-frying

◈

▲▲ Chop the hard-boiled eggs. Put the butter in a large bowl and heat on Full Power until melted (about 1 minute). Stir in the flour and cook until the roux puffs up (about 30 seconds). Stir in the milk and, without covering, cook, stirring occasionally, until the sauce thickens. Season with salt and pepper and add the mustard powder. Stir in the chopped eggs, nuts and parsley. Leave to cool.

◁ Divide the mixture into twelve pieces and roll into balls. Dip in the beaten egg and coat with the breadcrumbs. Cool in the refrigerator for 30 minutes.

Deep-fry a few at a time in hot oil, 190°C/360°F, making sure that the balls are fully immersed. Remove and drain on kitchen paper. Serve with mayonnaise.

AFRICAN QUEEN TART

This delicious tart has a meringue topping and a creamy filling. The pastry is made using the pineapple juice.

SERVES 6

◆

1 × 425 g/14 oz can crushed pineapple
170 g/6 oz self-raising flour
Pinch of salt
85 g/3 oz hard margarine
2 eggs
2 medium bananas
2 tablespoons arrowroot
1½-2 tablespoons pineapple juice from the can
215 ml/8 fl oz apricot juice
130 g/4½ oz caster sugar

◆

◀ Drain the pineapple and reserve the juice. To make the pastry, sift the flour and salt into a mixing bowl and rub in the margarine to fine crumb stage. Mix in sufficient pineapple juice to form a smooth dough. Roll out and fit into a greased 23 cm/9 inch shallow round glass dish. Line with foil and bake in a preheated 200°C/400°F/Gas Mark 6 oven for 15-20 minutes, removing the foil after 10 minutes.

▲▲ Separate the eggs. Mash the bananas with the yolks in a large bowl. Work in the arrowroot, pineapple pieces, apricot juice and 15 g/½ oz of sugar if liked. Without covering, cook on Full Power, stirring frequently, until the mixture thickens (about 5 minutes). Pour into the pastry case.

Using clean, grease-free beaters, whip the egg whites to stiff peaks. Add one-third of the remaining sugar and beat again until stiff. Fold in the remaining sugar. Spoon over the filling, smoothing the meringue to the sides. Without covering, cook until puffy (about 5 minutes). If the meringue cracks, coax it back into position during cooking.

◀ Briefly brown at a distance under a hot grill. Serve immediately.

APRICOT PUDDING

This nutty upside-down pudding is served with an apricot sauce.

SERVES 6

◆

55 g/2 oz hazelnuts
30 g/1 oz butter
45 g/1½ oz soft brown sugar
1 × 400 g/14 oz can apricot halves in natural juice
115 g/4 oz soft tub margarine
115 g/4 oz caster sugar
2 eggs
115 g/4 oz self-raising flour
1 teaspoon baking powder
2 tablespoons apricot jam
1 teaspoon lemon juice

◆

▲▲ Spread the hazelnuts on greaseproof paper on the microwave base. Without covering, cook on Full Power, stirring frequently, to toast the nuts (about 2 minutes). The only way to test for cooking is to cut one of the nuts in half to see whether it is brown inside. Rub between a folded sheet of kitchen paper to remove some of the skins. Finely chop or pulverize in a food processor.

Put the butter in a shallow 20 cm/8 inch round ovenglass dish. Without covering, heat until melted (about 1 minute). Stir in the brown sugar until dissolved. Drain the apricots, reserving the juice. Arrange cut side up on the syrupy base.

◀ Put the margarine, caster sugar, eggs, flour and baking powder in a mixing bowl and beat for 2 or 3 minutes until smooth and well aerated. Fold in the nuts and spread evenly over the apricots.

Bake in a preheated 180°C/350°F/Gas Mark 4 oven until well risen and firm to the touch (about 40 minutes).

▲▲ While the pudding is baking, put 140 ml/¼ pint of the apricot juice in a measuring jug. Stir in the jam and lemon juice and cook on Full Power until boiling (about 2 minutes). Stir and cook until slightly thick (about 4 minutes).

Turn out the pudding on to a heated serving dish and pour a little of the sauce over each portion.

ORANGE CREAM ÉCLAIRS

Ring the changes by altering the flavour of the filling and the icing.

MAKES 7 TO 10 ÉCLAIRS

◆

55 g/2 oz butter
140 ml/¼ pint water
70 g/2½ oz plain flour, sifted
Pinch of salt
2 eggs
140 ml/¼ pint double cream
2 tablespoons brandy
1 tablespoon caster sugar
115 g/4 oz icing sugar
1 tablespoon fresh orange juice
Orange food colouring (optional)

◆

▲▲ Put the butter and water in a medium bowl. Without covering, heat on Full Power until boiling (about 2 minutes). Immediately add the flour and salt and mix well. Without covering, cook until thick (about 30 seconds). Lightly beat the eggs and beat a little at a time into the paste. The mixture will appear slimy at first but becomes smooth and shiny after beating. Cover and set aside for 30 minutes.

◀ Spoon into a piping bag fitted with a 1 cm/½ inch plain nozzle and pipe 10 cm/4 inch lengths, well spaced out, onto greased baking sheets. Bake in a preheated 200°C/400°F/Gas Mark 6 oven until well risen, brown and crisp (about 20-25 minutes). Make a slit in the side of each to let the steam escape and return to the oven for a few minutes to dry out. Put on a rack to cool.

Beat the cream, brandy and caster sugar until thick. Spoon into the éclairs. Sieve the icing sugar into a bowl and work in the orange juice. Colour with orange food colouring if liked. Spread a teaspoon of icing over each éclair. Leave to set. Serve fresh.

RASPBERRY CHEESECAKE

A better and more luxurious cheesecake could not be purchased from any baker. The cake has a pastry base and the filling is generous with a topping of fresh raspberries set in redcurrant jelly.

SERVES 8 to 10

◆

Pastry base
85 g/3 oz butter
45 g/1½ oz caster sugar
2 digestive biscuits, well crushed
85 g/3 oz plain flour
Filling
225 g/8 oz cottage cheese
340 g/12 oz full cream cheese
85 g/3 oz caster sugar
2 eggs
1 teaspoon vanilla essence
Topping
225 g/8 oz raspberries
170 g/6 oz redcurrant jelly

◆

▲▲ To make the base, put the butter in a medium bowl. Without covering, heat on Full Power until melted (about 2 minutes). Stir in the sugar and biscuit crumbs. Mix in the flour until no white particles remain. Base line a 20 cm/8 inch round by 5 cm/2 inch deep dish with non-stick baking parchment. Press the mixture into the base and cover with greaseproof paper. Weigh down with baking beans. Without covering, cook until it is the texture of shortbread (about 3 minutes). Remove the paper and beans.

For the filling, blend the cheeses, sugar, eggs and vanilla essence in a food processor or liquidizer. Pour onto the base. Without covering, cook until the edges of the mixture are warm (about 1¾ minutes).

◀ Transfer to a preheated 180°C/350°F/Gas Mark 4 oven and bake until set and just colouring on top (about 20 minutes). Leave to cool then cover with raspberries.

▲▲ Put the redcurrant jelly in a jug and stir in 2 teaspoons of water. Without covering, heat on Full Power, stirring halfway through, until liquid (about 1½ minutes). Stir, then pour evenly over the raspberries. Chill for 30 minutes then serve from the dish.

RHUBARB LATTICE WITH VANILLA SAUCE

Take time to cut out and twist the pastry strips as the decorative lattice is so attractive. You will enjoy this even if you are not a rhubarb addict, and the sauce is light and delicate.

SERVES 4 to 6

❖

450 g/1 lb fresh rhubarb, trimmed
115 g/4 oz dark or soft brown sugar
55 g/2 oz sultanas
55 g/2 oz currants
55 g/2 oz raisins
55 g/2 oz chopped walnuts
½ teaspoon cinnamon
¼ teaspoon ground ginger
340 g/12 oz ready-to-roll shortcrust pastry
1 egg, beaten
Sauce
285 ml/½ pint milk
1 vanilla pod
4 teaspoons cornflour
30 g/1 oz caster sugar
1 teaspoon orange flower water
Knob of butter

❖

▲▲ Cut the rhubarb into 2.5 cm/1 inch lengths. Put in a large bowl and add the sugar, sultanas, currants, raisins, walnuts, cinnamon and ginger. Cover and cook on Full Power, stirring occasionally, until the rhubarb boils up but not over (about 5 minutes). Uncover and continue cooking, stirring occasionally, until mushy. Cover and leave to cool.

◀ Meanwhile, roll out three-quarters of the pastry and use to line a 23 cm/9 inch flan dish. Roll out the remaining pastry and cut into 23 × 1 cm/9 × ½ inch strips. Twist the strips, then chill both the pastry case and strips.

Fill the pastry case with cooked rhubarb. Dampen the ends of the pastry strips and use to make a lattice on the tart. Brush the strips with beaten egg. Bake in a preheated 200°C/400°F/Gas Mark 6 oven for 30-35 minutes.

▲▲ Make the sauce while the pastry is baking. Put the milk in a lipped bowl and add the vanilla pod. Without covering, cook on Full Power until steaming (about 2 minutes). Stir, then leave to stand for 10 minutes. Remove the vanilla pod. Blend the cornflour with 1 tablespoon of cold water and stir into the milk. Add the sugar and orange flower water. Without covering, cook, stirring occasionally, until the sauce thickens, then stir in the butter.

Serve the pie hot, lightly masked with the sauce.

TOSCA PEARS

This dessert is beloved by the Swedish and is now becoming popular world-wide.

SERVES 4 to 6

❖

55 g/2 oz butter
3 tablespoons caster sugar
1 tablespoon flour
1 tablespoon milk
55 g/2 oz flaked almonds
4-6 large firm dessert pears
Whipped cream to serve

❖

▲▲ Put the butter in a medium bowl and heat until melted (about 1 minute). Stir in the sugar, flour, flaked almonds and milk. Without covering, cook, stirring frequently, until thickened (about 2 minutes).

Peel and halve the pears lengthwise and scoop out the cores. Place, cut side up, in a single layer in a large shallow ovenproof dish. Without covering, cook on Full Power until the outer pears are hot (about 1½ minutes). Reposition the pears, placing those in the centre on the outside and cook until hot (about 1 minute). Spread the cooked mixture over the individual pear halves.

◀ Bake in a preheated 220°C/425°F/Gas Mark 7 oven, basting occasionally, until the pears are very tender but not mushy (about 20 minutes). Serve with freshly whipped cream.

STRAWBERRY GOUGÈRE

A ring of choux pastry is filled with fresh strawberries and whipped cream, then decorated with small choux buns and whole strawberries fixed with a little extra cream.

SERVES 6

◆

285 ml/½ pint water
55 g/2 oz butter
140 g/5 oz plain flour
4 eggs
450 g/1 lb strawberries
140 ml/¼ pint double cream
2 tablespoons caster sugar
Icing sugar

◆

▲▲ Put the water and butter in a medium bowl. Without covering, heat on Full Power until boiling (about 3 minutes). Stir and heat until boiling once more. Immediately add the flour all at once and beat until smooth. Replace in the microwave and, without covering, cook, beating occasionally, until the dough forms a soft ball (about 45 seconds). Beat the eggs and beat into the dough a little at a time. Continue beating until there is no separation. Put into a piping bag fitted with a plain 1 cm/½ inch nozzle.

◀ Line a baking tray with non-stick baking parchment. Pipe a thick border of the choux paste around in a 15 cm/6 inch circle. Pipe the remaining paste into five or six small balls, spacing these out at the sides of the tray. Bake in a preheated 220°C/425°F/Gas Mark 7 oven for about 20 minutes. Reduce the temperature to 190°C/375°F/Gas Mark 5 and bake until well risen, crisp and brown (about 20 minutes). Immediately split the pastry ring and buns with a sharp knife and scrape out any soft dough. Switch off the oven, then return the rings and bun halves to the oven and leave for 10 minutes to dry out. Leave until cold.

Reserve five or six well-shaped strawberries and slice the remainder. Whip the cream and caster sugar until thick. Fill the choux ring and buns with sliced strawberries and sweetened cream. Arrange the choux buns on top of the ring, fixing them with a little cream, then top with a dab of cream and a whole strawberry. Dust generously with icing sugar before serving.

FRUIT SLICES

This is one of my favourite recipes – the slices can be served hot or cold for tea, at coffee time or as a dessert.

MAKES 16 to 20

◆

450 g/1 lb ready-to-roll shortcrust pastry
115 g/4 oz butter
115 g/4 oz soft brown sugar
1 tablespoon golden syrup
450 g/1 lb mixed dried fruit
30 g/1 oz cornflour
½ teaspoon ground mixed spice
1 egg white
30 g/1 oz caster sugar

◆

▲▲ Grease the base and sides of a 28 cm × 20 cm/11 × 8 inch swiss roll tin well. Roll out half the pastry and use to line both base and sides. Roll the remaining pastry to a similar size. Chill both in the refrigerator.

Put the butter, brown sugar and syrup in a large bowl. Without covering, heat on Full Power, stirring occasionally, until melted (about 2 minutes). Mix the fruit, cornflour and spice together and stir into the syrup. Without covering, cook, stirring frequently, until boiling (about 4 minutes). Cook for a further 30 seconds. Leave to cool.

◀ Spread the filling over the pastry base, leaving a 1 cm/½ inch border. Dampen the edges, cover with the remaining pastry and press down well along the sides. Score the surface diagonally with a sharp knife. Brush with beaten egg white and dredge with caster sugar. Bake in a preheated 200°C/400°F/Gas Mark 6 oven until the top of the pastry is golden brown and the underside cooked (about 30 minutes).

Cut into bars while warm and remove from the tin.

Strawberry Gougère and Fruit Slices

BRANDIED CHERRY SOUFFLÉ

This is unbelievably delicious, and the layers remain attractive when the soufflé is served. Any leftovers can be served chilled.

SERVES 4

◈

3-4 tablespoons icing sugar
6 sponge finger biscuits
2 tablespoons sherry
16 glacé cherries
3 tablespoons brandy
15 g/½ oz butter
1 tablespoon flour
6 tablespoons milk
3 egg yolks, threads removed
1 tablespoon caster sugar
Few drops of almond essence
5 egg whites

◈

◀ Preheat the oven to 180°C/350°F/Gas Mask 4. Grease a 18 cm/7 inch soufflé dish and dust lightly with icing sugar. Spread the finger biscuits on a plate and pour over the sherry. Quarter the cherries and mix in a basin with 1 tablespoon of brandy.

▲▲ Heat the butter in a large bowl on Full Power until melted (about 20 seconds). Stir in the flour. Mix in the milk, egg yolks, caster sugar and almond essence and blend thoroughly. Without covering, cook until thickened, stirring frequently to prevent curdling (about 2 minutes). Take care not to overcook.

◀ Using clean, grease-free beaters, whip the egg whites to stiff peaks. Stir 1 tablespoon of beaten whites into the custard, then fold in the remainder. Pour half the mixture into the dish. Cover with sponge fingers and half the cherries. Pour in the remaining soufflé mixture and sift icing sugar thickly over the surface. Bake in the centre of the oven until risen and only just set (about 30 minutes). Scatter with the remaining cherries.

▲▲ Put 2 tablespoons of brandy in a mug and, without covering, heat on Full Power for 15-20 seconds only (have a match ready). Pour the brandy over the soufflé, strike the match and light the brandy. Serve immediately.

UNDERWOOD CRUMBLE

Leave this tart to cool a little before serving – the filling becomes very hot during cooking.

SERVES 4

◆

55 g/2 oz butter
115 g/4 oz self-raising flour
55 g/2 oz golden granulated sugar
½ teaspoon ground ginger
10 glacé cherries
55 g/2 oz chopped mixed peel
30 g/1 oz chopped angelica
Filling
85 g/3 oz butter
85 g/3 oz caster sugar
2 egg yolks

◆

▲▲ Cut up the butter and rub into the flour to resemble fine breadcrumbs. Stir in the granulated sugar and ginger. Press into the base and sides of a 18 cm/7 inch flan dish. Slice the cherries and mix with the peel and angelica. Spread on the base.

To make the filling, put the butter in a medium bowl and heat until soft (about 30 seconds). Mix in the caster sugar, then beat in the egg yolks. Without covering, cook on Defrost (35%), stirring frequently, until the mixture boils (about 6 minutes). Stir and pour the filling into the crumble case.

◀ Bake in a preheated 180°C/350°F/Gas Mark 4 oven until the crumble is cooked (about 25 minutes).

VALENCIA PUDDING

This is a meringue-topped franzipan pudding.

SERVES 4 to 6

◆

Pudding Base
425 ml/¾ pint milk
Few drops of almond essence
30 g/1 oz butter
30 g/1 oz caster sugar
55 g/2 oz fresh white breadcrumbs
30 g/1 oz ground almonds
2 teaspoons grated lemon rind
2 egg yolks
1 whole egg
3 tablespoons plum jam
Meringue Topping
2 egg whites
55 g/2 oz caster sugar
30 g/1 oz ground almonds

◆

▲▲ Put the milk in a medium bowl and, without covering, heat on Full Power until steaming but not boiling (about 2¼ minutes). Stir in the almond essence and butter until melted. Add the sugar, breadcrumbs, ground almonds and lemon rind. Leave to stand for 10 minutes to thicken up. Beat the yolks and the remaining whole egg into the pudding mixture. Pour into a greased 750 ml/1¼ pint pie dish.

◀ Bake in a preheated 180°C/350°F/Gas Mark 4 oven until firm (about 25 minutes). Leave the oven on.

▲▲ Put the jam on an undecorated saucer and, without covering, heat on Full Power until runny (about 30 seconds). Pour evenly over the pudding.

◀ To make the meringue, beat the egg whites to stiff peaks. Beat in half the caster sugar until stiff. Fold in the rest of the sugar and the ground almonds. Pile on top of the pudding and spread to the edges of the dish.

Return to the oven and bake until puffy and brown.

COCONUT FUDGE BARS

These are gorgeous but rich, so one will probably be sufficient for most people.

MAKES 16 to 18

◆

Base
115 g/4 oz flour, sifted
55 g/2 oz butter
55 g/2 oz caster sugar
1 egg yolk
¼ teaspoon almond essence
Filling
55 g/2 oz butter
1 × 285 ml/10 fl oz can condensed milk
2 tablespoons cocoa powder
85 g/3 oz desiccated coconut
Topping
170 g/6 oz milk or plain chocolate

◆

◀ Mix together the base ingredients to form a paste. Knead and roll out to an 18 × 23 cm/7 × 9 inch rectangle that is 5 mm/¼ inch thick. Place on a greased baking tray. Prick the base and bake in a preheated 180°C/350°F/Gas Mark 4 oven for about 15 minutes until golden. Leave in the tin to cool.

▲▲ To make the filling, put the butter in a medium bowl and, without covering, heat on Full Power until melted (about 30 seconds). Stir in the condensed milk and the cocoa powder. Without covering, heat until warm (about 30 seconds). Add the desiccated coconut. Mix well and spread over the baked base. Leave to cool.

Break the chocolate into squares. Put in a jug and, without covering, cook until shiny (about 1½ minutes). Stir until melted, then pour over the filling and leave to cool. Mark with a fork before the chocolate sets. When cool, divide into bars.

Store the bars in the refrigerator, interleaved with greaseproof paper.

BAKED CHOCALASKA

This is a variation on the baked Alaska theme.

SERVES 6

◆

70 g/2½ oz plain flour
½ teaspoon bicarbonate of soda
½ teaspoon baking powder
1 tablespoon cocoa
55 g/2 oz soft margarine
55 g/2 oz caster sugar
1 egg
1 tablespoon golden syrup
1 teaspoon Tia Maria
2 tablespoons milk
1 litre/1¾ pint block chocolate ice cream, halved
Meringue
4 egg whites
225 g/8 oz caster sugar

◆

▲▲ Sift the flour, bicarbonate of soda, baking powder and cocoa together. Beat the margarine and sugar until fluffy. Beat the egg lightly and gradually stir into the mixture. Mix in the flour mixture. Add the golden syrup, liqueur and milk and beat to a smooth thick batter.

Grease a 20 × 28 cm/8 × 11 inch dish well and line the base with greased greaseproof paper. Pour in the batter and, without covering, cook on Full Power until just dry on top (about 3 minutes). Leave to stand for 5 minutes, then loosen the edges and turn on to a wire rack. Leave until cool. Wrap in cling film and freeze until firm (about 1 hour). Wash and chill the baking tray.

◄ Preheat the oven to 230°C/450°F/Gas Mark 8. To make the meringue, beat the egg whites until stiff. Gradually beat in half the sugar until stiff peaks form, fold in the remaining sugar and place in a piping bag fitted with a 1 cm/½ inch star nozzle. Unwrap the cake base and place on the greased baking tray. Place the ice cream blocks side by side in the middle of the cake. Pipe the meringue thickly over the ice cream, making sure it reaches the edges of the cake.

Bake in the centre of the preheated oven until the meringue is brown (about 5 minutes). Serve immediately.

Almond and Apple Pancakes (*see page 72*) and Baked Chocalaska

ALMOND AND APPLE PANCAKES

Make ahead of time and freeze the pancakes and filling separately, then assemble after thawing and finish under a hot grill.

SERVES 6 TO 8

◆

Pancake batter
225 g/8 oz plain flour
¼ teaspoon salt
2 eggs
About 570 ml/1 pint milk
Filling
450 g/1 lb cooking apples
Grated rind and juice of ½ lemon
55 g/2 oz caster sugar
½ teaspoon ground cinnamon
30 g/1 oz butter
30 g/1 oz ground almonds
30 g/1 oz raisins
1 tablespoon apricot jam
55 g/2 oz flaked almonds
Icing sugar

◆

◀ To make the pancakes, sieve the flour and salt into the mixing bowl, make a well in the centre and add the eggs and half the milk. Gradually incorporate the flour, stirring all the time. As soon as the batter becomes thick, add the remaining milk. Beat with a whisk to form a smooth batter of thin pouring consistency. Leave to stand for 30 minutes, then adjust the consistency if necessary by adding more milk.

Heat a small heavy-based frying pan. Grease the surface and pour in about 1 tablespoon of batter. Tilt the handle to evenly spread the batter and cook for ½-1 minute until the underside is brown and the surface is opaque. Loosen the pancake with a palette knife and turn over to cook the other side. Turn out and grease the pan again if necessary before adding more batter. Stack the pancakes between sheets of greaseproof paper.

▲▲ To make the filling, peel, core and slice the apples. Mix with the lemon rind and juice, sugar and cinnamon in a large bowl. Add the butter, cover and cook on Full Power, stirring occasionally, until the apples are tender (about 4 minutes). Mix in the ground almonds and raisins. Spoon a little of the filling in the centre of each pancake and fold it over.

◀ Arrange in a single layer in a flameproof dish. Dot with jam and sprinkle with flaked almonds. Brown under a hot grill, sprinkle with icing sugar and serve hot.

GINGER CRISP BISCUITS

These will need to be stored in an airtight container to ensure their crispness.

MAKES 16

◆

85 g/3 oz butter
1 tablespoon golden syrup
Pinch of bicarbonate of soda
1 teaspoon ground ginger
85 g/3 oz caster sugar
170 g/6 oz self-raising flour

◆

▲▲ Put the butter and syrup in a medium bowl and heat on Full Power, stirring frequently, until melted (about 1 minute). Mix in the bicarbonate of soda, ginger and sugar, then work in the flour to a soft dough. Shape into sixteen even-sized balls.

◀ Spread the balls out on a baking tray and press down lightly with a fork. The cookies spread during baking so it is important to space them out. Bake in a preheated 190°C/375°F/Gas Mark 5 oven until golden brown (about 12 minutes). Lift from the baking tray with a fish slice and cool on a wire rack.

LEMON ALMOND OATCAKE

This is a sort of flapjack, but with more the texture of a cake.

MAKES ABOUT 16

❖

115 g/4 oz butter
2 tablespoons golden syrup
115 g/4 oz caster sugar
225 g/8 oz porridge oats
55 g/2 oz ground almonds
30 g/1 oz flaked almonds
Grated rind and juice of ½ lemon
115 g/4 oz icing sugar
Yellow food colouring

❖

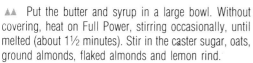 Put the butter and syrup in a large bowl. Without covering, heat on Full Power, stirring occasionally, until melted (about 1½ minutes). Stir in the caster sugar, oats, ground almonds, flaked almonds and lemon rind.

Grease and line an 18 × 25 cm/7 × 10 inch shallow tin with non-stick baking parchment. Spoon in the cake mixture and smooth the surface. Bake in a preheated 180°C/350°F/Gas Mark 4 oven until light brown (about 15 minutes). Leave to cool.

Put the lemon juice in a bowl and gradually blend in enough icing sugar to form a thick icing. Add food colouring if liked. Spoon a thin layer of icing over the oatcake. Leave until set. Cut into bars or squares to serve.

BRANDY SNAPS

These crispy mouthwatering brandy snaps are filled with whipped brandied cream and dipped in chopped angelica. Make them the usual way or shape the scrumptious biscuits around cream horn cornet moulds.

SERVES 6

❖

85 g/3 oz butter
85 g/3 oz golden syrup
170 g/6 oz caster sugar
Grated rind of 1 lemon
85 g/3 oz flour
1 teaspoon ground ginger
4 teaspoons brandy
285 ml/½ pint double cream
1 tablespoon icing sugar
3 tablespoons chopped angelica

❖

Oil the handles of two large wooden spoons. Combine the butter, syrup, sugar and lemon rind in a medium bowl, and cook on Full Power, stirring frequently, until dissolved (about 3 minutes). Stir in the flour and ginger and 1 teaspoon of brandy. Beat until smooth.

Line two baking trays with non-stick baking parchment. Space out well four rounded teaspoons of the mixture on each tray. Bake one tray at a time in a preheated 160°C/325°F/Gas Mark 3 oven until the biscuits spread thinly and are golden (about 5-7 minutes). Leave for 20 seconds.

Coil the biscuits one at a time around the spoon handles, letting each slip down towards the bowl of the spoon. If the mixture in the bowl cools and dries, put in the microwave to soften (about 20 seconds). While baking the second batch, slip the brandy snaps off the spoon handle and cool on a wire rack. Complete baking the remaining brandy snaps in the same way. Leave until cold. Store in an airtight container until required.

Beat the cream, sugar and remaining brandy together until stiff. Spoon into either end of the brandy snaps and lightly dip each in chopped angelica.

Haute cuisine and the microwave can be synonymous, provided that the basic techniques have been mastered first. Base your menu on the recipes in this chapter, then have a look through your own favourite dinner party recipes and adapt those that the microwave will not only be able to cope with but do well.

Among these you should be able to select soups that need no pre-frying purées and soups thickening with a beurre manié or egg/cream liaison are always successful. Start with a smaller quantity of liquid than you would need conventionally, adding more towards the end of cooking. As cooking is quicker, there will be far less evaporation. You may find that seasonings need to be adjusted accordingly; although lengthy cooking develops flavour, you will still need less herbs in the smaller amount of liquid.

Vegetable starters, such as globe artichokes, fresh asparagus and Mushrooms à la Grèque, should be included in your repertoire. Pâtés and mousses are a must, but large, course terrines are better left to conventional methods.

Whenever a recipe calls for poached or steamed fish, use the microwave and garnish with sauces, which are one of the areas where the microwave excels. These can be cooked in with the fish or prepared by microwave for serving separately. Shellfish is also a must in the microwave, but, of course, you will not be able to tackle dishes like breaded scampi as you cannot fry in a microwave.

Microwaving is a much healthier form of cooking as fat in meat and poultry simply oozes out, so you do not need to use so much fat for cooking. Remove all visible fat from joints or cuts of meat before cooking and baste away the melted fat as it gathers. Skin chicken pieces before cooking or you will have to spoon a fatty layer from the surface of casseroles.

It goes without saying that good-quality ingredients make good-quality dishes. This is particularly true as far as meat is concerned. The microwave cannot tenderize as the right conditions are not created to do this. Although microwaves are mainly attracted to water, even when there is a substantial quantity liquid such as in a casserole, some microwave friction occurs within the meat. So although the meat will cook satisfactorily in some people's view, it will not become soft – the texture will remain reminiscent of grilled steak. However: meat that has been tenderized prior to cooking turns out very well. To tenderize, either marinate, chop, mince, beat or treat with tenderizing powder – an enzyme from the papaya.

Among the successful desserts are purées, fools, compôtes and all recipes that have fruit as their chief ingredient. Mousses made with gelatine or fluffed up with egg white, custards, ice cream and sponge puddings all come out superbly when cooked in the microwave. A sweet sauce improves any plain pudding and most can be adapted from your own well-thumbed cookbook.

To end your meal treat your guests with a sweetmeat, dinner mint or truffle and an Irish coffee – all prepared so easily by microwave.

MICROWAVE PARTY DISHES

CHAPTER 4

AUBERGINE VÉGÉTARIENNE

Look out for small, well-shaped, unblemished aubergines. This recipe was primarily conceived for vegetarians who are so often served with monotonous dishes, but cooked minced meat could be substituted for the kidney beans. Double the recipe if more servings are required and reheat in two batches.

SERVES 4

◆

4 × 170 g/6 oz aubergines
4-5 tablespoons water
½ bunch spring onions
1 tablespoons salad oil
1 × 213 g/7½ oz can kidney beans
Salt and freshly milled black pepper
4 tablespoons Cheddar cheese, grated

◆

To make sure of a good balance, first sit the aubergines on a work surface, placing them in the steadiest position. Remove a thin slice along the tops to serve as a lid. Replace the aubergine lids and put the vegetables in a single layer in a large shallow dish, adding the water. Cover tightly and cook on Full Power until soft (about 10 minutes).

While the aubergines are cooking, finely slice the spring onions and put in a dish with the oil. Stir briefly and, without covering, cook until soft (about 2 minutes).

Remove the aubergines from the dish, scoop the pulp from the base and lid and finely chop. Drain and rinse the kidney beans. Mix the aubergine pulp, onions and beans together and mash lightly so that most of the beans are broken. Season with salt and pepper. Mix in the grated cheese. Put the aubergine shells back into the dish and pack with the filling. Replace the aubergine lids. Without covering, cook to reheat, repositioning the aubergines once during cooking (about 6 minutes).

CHICKEN LIVER AND GREEN OLIVE PÂTÉ

Chicken livers pop and splatter during cooking, leave for a few seconds in between each stirring and also before liquidizing. The recipe may be doubled – only 3 more minutes cooking will be required. Black olives or capers may be substituted for the green olives, and a dash of brandy will improve the keeping qualities. The pâté may be frozen but this will soften the olives.

SERVES 4 to 6

◆

225 g/8 oz chicken livers
1 small onion
1 small clove garlic
8 pitted green olives
115 g/4 oz butter
½ teaspoon dried marjoram
2 teaspoons dry sherry
2 teaspoons port
Salt and freshly milled black pepper
Garnish
Finely chopped parsley

◆

Trim, rinse and halve the chicken livers. Peel, quarter and slice the onion. Peel the garlic. Slice the olives wafer thin. Put 30 g/1 oz of butter in a large bowl and add the onion and garlic. Without covering, cook on Full Power, stirring occasionally, until the onion is translucent (about 2 minutes). Stir in the chicken livers and marjoram, cover and cook, stirring occasionally, until the livers are just pink inside (about 3 minutes).

Blend the mixture in a liquidizer (not a food processor) at the same time adding the remaining butter, sherry and port. Season to taste. Spread one-third of the pâté into a 285 ml/½ pint pâté dish, cover with a layer of olive slices, then build up with a further layer of pâté and olives and finish with a topping of pâté. Smooth the top carefully with the back of a spoon and sprinkle with chopped parsley. Chill in the refrigerator for 2-3 hours before serving.

GÂTEAU ÉPINARDS

Use fresh or frozen spinach, but try not to use the canned variety as it will spoil the colour and tastes slightly bitter. I discovered that fresh spinach was not a particular bargain, since 450 g/1 lb when drained and chopped yields only 255 g/9 oz. The laborious task of cutting circles from non-stick parchment can be avoided by purchasing packets of discs in varying sizes – if you cannot find them in the shops, they can be ordered by mail order from Lakeland Plastics, Windermere.

SERVES 4 to 5

◈

55 g/2 oz cashew nuts
115 g/ oz soft cream cheese
1 tablespoon milk
3 large eggs, separated
¼ teaspoon salt
115 g/4 oz drained cooked spinach, chopped
Freshly milled black pepper
¼ teaspoon grated nutmeg
1 tablespoon cornflour

◈

Grease a deep, 15 cm/6 inch round, glass cake dish and line the base with a non-stick parchment disc. Reserve a few cashew nuts and finely grate the remainder. Blend the cheese, grated nuts and milk together and set aside.

Whisk the egg yolks and salt until thick. Beat in the chopped spinach and season with pepper and the nutmeg, then sprinkle with the cornflour sieved through a strainer. Using clean beaters, whisk the egg whites to soft peaks. Fold into the spinach mixture using a large metal spoon to maintain sufficient aeration. Pour half the mixture into the prepared dish. Without undue pressure, place a 18 cm/ 7 inch non-stick parchment disc on top. Pour on the remaining mixture. The disc will be sandwiched in the middle.

Without covering, cook on Defrost (35%) until just set (about 10 minutes). Turn out onto a heated serving dish and separate the cake layers. Spread one half with cheese mixture and sandwich with the remaining cake. Spread the top and sides with the remaining cheese. Decorate with the reserved nuts.

Serve preferably hot. Any leftovers can be eaten cold or briefly reheated on Defrost (35%), however the texture will be tougher.

LIME AND AVOCADO MOUSSE

This refreshing starter is ideal for a summer evening. Serve as part of a buffet supper or garnished with salad ingredients at a dinner party.

SERVES 4 to 5

◈

1 lime
2 teaspoons powdered gelatine
½ teaspoon icing sugar
2 ripe avocados
4 tablespoons natural yogurt
Salt and pepper
Garnish
Thinly cut slices of cucumber, small, centre lettuce leaves, button tomatoes

◈

Grate the rind and squeeze the juice from the lime. Set aside 1 tablespoon of the juice and put the remainder into a large measuring jug with the rind. Make up to 140 ml/¼ pint with cold water. Stir in the gelatine and sugar. Without covering, cook on Full Power until hot (about 1 minute). Stir until all crystals are dissolved. Leave in a cool place until just beginning to set.

Peel and stone the avocados and blend the flesh with the gelatine mixture in a food processor or liquidizer. Add the yogurt and seasoning and blend briefly. Pour into a 425 ml/¾ pint pâté dish. Sprinkle with the reserved lime juice and chill in the refrigerator for about 2 hours.

Garnish with cucumber slices and serve on a bed of fresh green lettuce leaves topped with the quartered tomatoes.

ARTICHOKES BÉARNAISE

Artichokes are an interesting starter, but should be followed by a stronger-flavoured main course. Serve dressed with vinaigrette or melted butter, Hollandaise or Béarnaise sauce.

SERVES 4

◆

4 globe artichokes
285 ml/½ pint hot water
1 teaspoon lemon juice
Sauce
1 shallot
85 g/3 oz unsalted butter
3 tablespoons tarragon vinegar
Pinch of salt
1 tablespoon freshly chopped chervil
2 egg yolks
Garnish
Lemon wedges

◆

To prepare the artichokes, remove the tips and open out the leaves. Using a small, sharp knife, cut out and discard the hairy choke from the centre. Wash the artichokes thoroughly in cold water and reshape. Stir the water and lemon juice together in a very large casserole or bowl and put in the artichokes. Cover tightly and cook on Full Power until the parts towards the outside are tender (about 10 minutes). Reposition and turn the artichokes over. Cover and cook until tender: an indication is when a leaf pulls away easily (about 10 minutes). Leave to stand covered for 5-10 minutes before draining.

To make the sauce, peel and very finely chop the shallot and put into a large basin with 15 g/½ oz of butter. Cover and cook, stirring once during cooking, until the shallot is soft (about 2 minutes). Stir in the vinegar, salt and a little of the chervil. Without covering, continue cooking until the liquid is reduced to only 1 teaspoonful (about 3 minutes). Meanwhile, beat the eggs and strain into a medium bowl. Beat vigorously with an electric whisk until frothy. Add the remaining butter to the shallot mixture. Without covering, cook until the butter is melted (about 1 minute). Re-cover and cook until bubbling (about 1 minute), then uncover and, while whisking the egg yolks furiously, pour the butter mixture in a steady stream over the beaters. This is the most important stage and you will need both hands for the job. Fold in the remaining chervil.

Serve the artichokes on individual heated plates, the sauce in the centre, and garnish with lemon wedges.

SMOKED SALMON MOUSSE

This slightly less expensive starter contains halibut fillet which adds bulk without detracting from the flavour of the smoked salmon.

SERVES 4 to 6

◆

225 g/8 oz halibut fillet
¼ teaspoon *quatre épices*
1 sprig parsley
1 bay leaf
1 tablespoon powdered gelatine
170 g/6 oz smoked salmon cocktail pieces
Juice of ½ medium lemon (1 tablespoon)
Sea salt and freshly milled black pepper
285 ml/½ pint whipping cream
2 egg whites
1 box mustard and cress

◆

Remove the skin and any stray bones from the halibut and put them in a medium jug. Add the spice, parsley and bay leaf, cover with water and cook on Full Power until the water boils (about 3 minutes). Reduce the setting to Defrost (35%) and cook for a further 10 minutes. Strain into a bowl and discard the skin and flavourings. Put 6 tablespoons of the fish liquor into the jug and stir in the gelatine. Without covering, cook on Full Power until bubbling (about 30 seconds). Set aside.

Discard all but 1 tablespoon of the remaining fish liquor and put the fish in the bowl, cutting up if necessary. Cover and cook on Full Power until white and flaky (about 2 minutes). Leave to cool. Put the salmon pieces, halibut, lemon juice and a generous seasoning of black pepper in a food processor or liquidizer and add the dissolved gelatine. Process until smooth. Pour in the cream and process until blended. Add salt if necessary. Separately beat the egg whites until stiff. Stir 1 tablespoon of the beaten whites into the smooth pâté, then fold in the remainder with a large metal spoon.

Rinse and dry the cress. Lightly grease one large or four to six small ramekin dishes and press the cress into the base and sides. Spoon in the mousse. Chill in the refrigerator for 2-3 hours or freeze if preferred.

To serve, gently dip the base(s) of the dish(es) in warm water, loosen around the sides with a round table knife and turn out onto a serving platter. Garnish with lemon peel or butter curls and Melba toast.

Artichokes Béarnaise and Smoked Salmon Mousse

BRIDGE CROÛTONS

These can be stored in a screw top jar or in the freezer, and are suitable as accompaniments to most soups.

SERVES 4 to 6

◆

**4 slices thin cut bread
2 tablespoons salad oil
¼ teaspoon paprika
¼ teaspoon grated Parmesan cheese**

◆

Using aspic cutters, cut out as many small shapes as possible from the bread but do not cut into the crusts. Put the oil into a shallow glass pie dish and, without covering, cook on Full Power until hot (about 1½ minutes). Stir in the paprika and Parmesan, add the bread pieces and toss so that they are completely coated. Without covering, cook, stirring frequently, until the croûtons are golden (about 3 minutes). Do not overcook or the croûtons will burn. Remove with a fish slice or slotted spoon and drain on kitchen paper. Serve hot.

If you wish, leave the croûtons until cool, then store in an airtight jar or in a closed container in the freezer. To reheat, spread the croûtons on kitchen paper and allow about 30 seconds on Full Power.

COARSE SPINACH SOUP

As this title suggests, this is a coarse soup. If you prefer to have a smoother soup, purée in a liquidizer or blender.

SERVES 4 to 5

◆

**1 medium onion
1 clove garlic
30 g/1 oz butter
30 g/1 oz flour
425 ml/¾ pint milk
340 g/12 oz frozen spinach, chopped
Salt and pepper**

◆

Finely chop the onion. Crush the garlic. Put the butter in a large bowl and heat on Full Power until melted (about 45 seconds). Stir in the onion and garlic. Cover and cook, stirring occasionally, until soft (about 5 minutes). Stir in the flour and add the milk. Without covering, cook, stirring frequently with a wire whisk, until the sauce thickens (about 5 minutes).

Thaw the spinach (covered) in a bowl, breaking off lumps as soon as possible (about 5 minutes). Chop finely with kitchen scissors. Mix into the sauce. Without covering, cook, stirring occasionally, until the spinach is soft (about 5 minutes). Season to taste with salt and pepper. Serve hot.

CAULIFLOWER AND BROCCOLI SOUP

This unusual soup has a charming flavour yet uses basic ingredients. The recipe can be halved if wished, in which case the cooking times must be reduced by about one-third. The soup can also be frozen, but will need blending before serving. Frozen vegetables are equally good, but allow extra time during initial cooking.

SERVES 8 to 10

❖

450 g/1 lb cauliflower florets
450 g/1 lb broccoli spears
30 g/1 oz butter
1 teaspoon tarragon leaves
570 ml/1 pint milk
570 ml/1 pint hot chicken stock or water and chicken stock cube
1 tablespoon cornflour
2 tablespoons salad oil
Salt and white pepper

❖

Put the cauliflower florets, broccoli spears, butter and tarragon leaves in a large bowl. Cover with a plate and cook on Full Power until soft, stirring occasionally (about 10 minutes for fresh and 20 minutes for frozen vegetables). Purée in a liquidizer with sufficient milk to allow the liquidizer to work properly. Pour back into the bowl and add the remaining milk and stock. Cover and cook until boiling (about 8 minutes). Stir and, without covering, bring back to the boil (about 5 minutes).

While the soup is heating, blend the cornflour and oil together in a small bowl. Add the blended cornflour in small amounts to the boiling soup and beat in with a wire whisk. Season to taste. Bring back to the boil (about 5 minutes). Stir. Bring back to the boil once more (about 3 minutes) before serving.

COURGETTE AND WATERCRESS SOUP

This pale green, smooth, creamy soup should be served in fairly small portions. To avoid a bitter taste, choose firm crisp courgettes.

SERVES 6 to 8

❖

1 small onion
1 clove garlic
680 g/1½ lb firm courgettes
1 bunch watercress
1 tablespoon salad oil
285 ml/½ pint water
¼ vegetable stock cube
Sea salt and freshly milled black pepper
285 ml/½ pint milk
1 egg yolk

❖

Slice the onion. Peel the garlic. Top, tail and slice the courgettes. Remove the watercress stalks.

Mix the onion, garlic and oil in a large bowl. Cover and cook on Full Power, stirring occasionally, until soft (about 5 minutes). Stir in the courgettes and all but twenty of the watercress leaves. Cover and cook until the courgettes are soft (about 10 minutes).

Purée in a liquidizer (not in a food processor which would be too coarse), adding half the water. Pour back into the bowl, add the remaining water and stock cube. Without covering, bring to the boil (about 6 minutes). Stir and test the consistency – if too thick, add a further 140 ml/¼ pint of water. Without covering, cook until boiling (about 3 minutes). Stir and season to taste.

Beat the milk and egg yolk together and strain into the soup. Without covering, cook, beating every 30 seconds, until the soup is reheated and smooth (about 2 minutes). Garnish with the reserved watercress leaves.

Tomato and Coriander Soup, Celeriac and Stilton Soup and Bridge Croûtons (*see page 80*)

CELERIAC AND STILTON SOUP

If you wish, you can cook this recipe in stages in advance. To do this, cook the celeriac, then peel and purée with the spring onions. Prepare the white sauce. Make the croûtons. All can be stored separately in the freezer for a few days. Extra water may be needed when completing the soup.

SERVES 4 to 6

◆

1 × 450-680 g/1-1½ lb celeriac
½ bunch spring onions
30 g/1 oz butter or margarine
30 g/1 oz flour
570 ml/1 pint milk
Salt and freshly milled black pepper
425-570 ml/¾-1 pint water
55 g/2 oz white Stilton cheese
20 Bridge Croûtons (see page 80)

◆

Scrub the celeriac. Trim the spring onions but do not remove the green part. Slice finely. Put the celeriac into a large bowl and add enough water to reach halfway up the sides of the vegetable (about 285 ml/½ pint). Cover with an inverted plate and cook on Full Power until the water boils (about 3 minutes). Carefully remove the plate and turn the celeriac over. Cover and cook until a fork can be easily inserted into the centre (about 10 minutes). Leave to stand covered while making the sauce. During this time the celeriac will cook further.

To make the sauce, put the butter or margarine in a large bowl. Without covering, heat on Full Power until just melted (about 30 seconds). Stir in the flour and, without covering, cook until the colour changes and seems to be dry (about 30 seconds). Add the milk all at once and mix with a wire whisk. Without covering, cook until the milk is hot (about 2 minutes). Beat with the whisk and continue cooking, beating every minute, until the sauce thickens to the consistency of cream (about 3 minutes). Beat again when cooking is complete.

Drain the celeriac and using a fork and sharp knife peel on a wooden board to prevent the vegetable from slipping. Cut up the flesh and purée with the onions and sauce in a liquidizer or blender. Season to taste. Pour into a large bowl and stir in 425 ml/¾ pint water. Partly cover and cook until boiling (about 5 minutes). Stir and, without covering, reheat until bubbles reappear (about 1 minute). Crumble in the Stilton and, without covering, heat, stirring occasionally, until well blended (about 4 minutes). Thin down with extra boiling water if necessary.

Heat the croûtons on a dish lined with kitchen paper (about 30 seconds), then sprinkle onto the individual soup portions.

TOMATO AND CORIANDER SOUP

This quick and easy soup has a remarkably delicate flavour imparted by the fresh coriander leaves. Do not use dried coriander if it can be avoided. Canned, bottled or long-life tomato juice are all suitable, but liquidized and strained fresh tomatoes can be used instead when cheap and plentiful, and this produces a slightly different flavour.

SERVES 4 to 5

◆

6 or 7 coriander leaves
55 g/2 oz mange-tout, fresh or thawed
1 medium carrot
570 ml/1 pint tomato juice
285 ml/½ pint water
Sea salt and freshly milled black pepper
55 g/2 oz fresh beansprouts

◆

Finely shred the coriander leaves with scissors. Thinly slice the mange-tout. Scrape and grate the carrot.

Put the coriander leaves and grated carrot in a large bowl and stir in the tomato juice and water. Cover and cook on Full Power until fast boiling around the edges (about 8 minutes). Stir in the mange-tout and season to taste.

Without covering, cook until the soup is fast boiling again (about 2 minutes). Stir in the beansprouts just before serving.

SOLE BONNE FEMME

Fish heads and bones are very heavy and can account for three-quarters of the bought weight. To obtain 680 g/1½ lb filletted skinned fish, you may need to purchase 2.25 kg/ 5 lb of fresh fish. However the trimmings can be used to make stock for a fish soup. The thickness of the sauce in this recipe will vary according to the size of mushrooms that you use – smaller mushrooms give less liquid. If necessary, adjust the consistency with fish stock.

SERVES 6

◆

680 g/1½ lb skinned lemon sole fillets, plus bones and skin from the fish
Squeeze of fresh lemon juice
Salt and freshly milled black pepper
1 bay leaf
30 g/1 oz butter
15 g/½ oz flour
450 g/1 lb button mushrooms
2 tablespoons freshly chopped parsley
1 egg yolk
140 ml/¼ pint double cream

◆

Sprinkle the fish on both sides with lemon juice and season with salt and pepper. Cut up the bones and put with the skins and bay leaf in a very large bowl. Just cover with water and, without covering further, cook on Full Power until the liquid boils up (about 10 minutes). Reduce the setting to Defrost (35%) and cook for about 10 minutes. Strain into a large measuring jug.

Put 15 g/½ oz of butter in a large deep dish. Without covering, heat on Full Power until melted (about 30 seconds), then stir in the flour. Whisk in 140 ml/¼ pint of the fish liquor and, without covering, cook, whisking frequently, until thickened (about 1 minute). Whisk again. Finely slice the mushrooms and stir into the sauce with the parsley. Cover and cook until the mushrooms are tender (about 5 minutes).

Arrange the fish fillets on top of the mushrooms, folding each in half. Cover and cook until the fish is white and flaky (about 5 minutes). Transfer both the fish and mushrooms to a heated and covered serving dish.

Blend the egg yolk and cream together. Stir into the liquor remaining in the dish and cook to thicken slightly (about 20 seconds). Season. Stir in the remaining butter and cook to thicken further, whisking occasionally (about 1½ minutes).

Pour the sauce over the food and serve at once.

COQUILLES ST. JACQUES ASPERGES

Use fresh or frozen scallops and, if using the latter, allow extra cooking time.

SERVES 6

◆

680 g/1½ lb frozen or trimmed scallops
1 × 340 g/12 oz can aparagus tips
About 140 ml/¼ pint medium white wine
½ teaspoon lemon juice
2 bay leaves
Salt and freshly milled black pepper
55 g/2 oz butter
45 g/1½ oz flour
140 ml/¼ pint single cream

◆

Halve the scallops and set aside. Strain and measure the asparagus liquor and make up to 285 ml/½ pint with the wine. Add the lemon juice, bay leaves, salt and pepper to taste. Pour into a large bowl and, without covering, cook on Full Power until the liquid is boiling (about 2½ minutes). Stir in the scallops and, without covering, cook until the liquid returns to the boil (about 1 minute). By this time the scallops should be opaque and no extra cooking should be necessary. Remove the scallops with a slotted spoon and keep warm.

Blend the butter and flour to a smooth paste. Stir into the cooking liquor in small amounts, beating constantly with a whisk. Without covering, cook the sauce, beating occasionally, until thickened (about 1½ minutes). Fold in the scallops and, without covering, reheat (about 30 seconds). Stir in the cream and, without covering, reheat (not more than 30 seconds). Stir, cover and keep warm.

Arrange the asparagus tips in a shallow dish. Cover and cook until hot (about 1 minute).

Serve the scallops and sauce in individual dishes and garnish with the asparagus tips.

THE MICROWAVE KITCHEN

NOISETTES DE SAUMON ET CREVETTES

The salmon cutlets are stuffed with a prawn filling and rolled up to resemble slices of swiss roll. Choose salmon with the underside unsevered, otherwise it will be difficult to keep the fish intact. The quantity can be increased, but extra cooking time will be needed. Serve with boiled new potatoes and mange-tout.

SERVES 4 to 6

680 g/1½ lb middle cut fresh salmon
Squeeze of fresh lemon juice
Salt and pepper
115 g/4 oz frozen shelled prawns, thawed
1 egg
2 tablespoons freshly chopped parsley
2 tablespoons mayonnaise
1 teaspoon tomato ketchup
4 tablespoons fresh white breadcrumbs

Cut the salmon into four or six steaks. Remove the bones. Using a sharp knife, remove the skin without severing the flesh at the loop end. Put the bones and skin and a squeeze of lemon juice in a large jug and add water to cover. Without covering further, cook on Full Power until boiling (about 3 minutes). Stir. Reduce the setting to Defrost (35%) and cook to develop the flavour (about 10 minutes). Season with salt and pepper.

Roughly chop the prawns and mix with the egg, parsley, mayonnaise, ketchup and breadcrumbs. Open out the salmon portions and spread with the filling. Roll up and arrange, cut side uppermost, in a large shallow dish. Strain on sufficient fish liquor to just moisten, cover with greaseproof paper and cook on Defrost (35%), repositioning the noisettes twice during cooking (about 15 minutes). If in doubt, slightly undercook because salmon tends to cook further when left to stand. Should reheating be intended, reduce the initial cooking time by 5 minutes.

BEEF ÉSCABÊCHE

Beef that has been marinated will be more tender since the oil and acid in the marinade break down the tough structure. To save vital time when preparing a dinner party, marinate the beef ahead of time and freeze in the marinade for up to 1 month. Choose a lean tender cut of meat if possible.

SERVES 5 to 6

1 large onion
1 clove garlic
680 g/1½ lb lean beef, preferably frying steak
3 tablespoons olive oil
3 tablespoons dry white wine
1 tablespoon white wine vinegar
4 bay leaves, crumbled
Salt and freshly milled black pepper
1 tablespoon flour
140 ml/¼ pint sweet red wine
2 teaspoons tomato purée

Thinly slice the onion. Peel and crush the garlic. Cut the meat into 1 cm/½ inch cubes. Mix the onion, garlic and oil in a very large bowl. Cover and cook on Full Power, stirring occasionally, until the onion is soft (about 10 minutes). Add the wine, vinegar and bay leaves and season lightly with salt and pepper. Mix in the cubed beef, cover and leave to marinate for 24 hours. Stir occasionally during this time.

Put the flour on a plate or piece of non-stick baking parchment and, without covering, cook on Full Power, stirring frequently, until the flour begins to brown (about 2½ minutes). Stir into the meat and marinade and add the red wine and tomato purée. Cover and cook on Full Power, stirring occasionally, until the meat is hot (about 10 minutes). Reduce the setting to Defrost (35%) and cook for a further 20 minutes. Season to taste with salt and pepper and continue cooking until the meat is tender (about 20 minutes).

Serve with spring greens or Brussels sprouts and mashed potatoes.

85

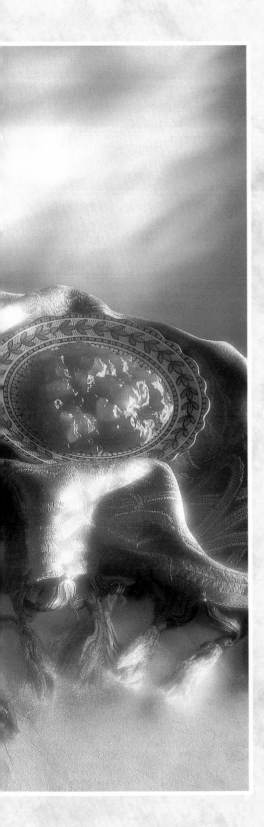

CURRIED BEEF
WITH TROPICAL FRUIT

This is a real show-stopper. It has a Caribbean air about it and is a most attractive way of serving curried meat balls. Serve with a crisp green salad and boiled rice if wished.

SERVES 6

◆

Meat balls
1 tablespoon curry powder
1 teaspoon vegetable oil
680 g/1½ lb minced lean raw beef
1 tablespoon Besan flour
Salt and black pepper
Sauce
225 g/8 oz onions
2 tablespoons vegetable oil
1 teaspoon ground cumin
1 teaspoon ground cardamom
1 teaspoon salt
1 teaspoon turmeric
¼ teaspoon mustard powder
¼ teaspoon ground ginger
¼ teaspoon ground cinnamon
½ teaspoon lemon juice
1 × 400 g/14 oz can chopped tomatoes
285 ml/½ pint water
1 tablespoon Besan flour
Fruit garnish
1 large pineapple
1 mango
6 kumquats
2 tablespoons mango chutney
Thickening
140 ml/¼ pint plain yogurt
1 tablespoon cornflour

◆

To make the meat balls, put the curry powder in a large bowl and, without covering, cook on Full Power until a roasted aroma is emitted (about 30 seconds). Stir in the oil, beef, Besan flour and a light seasoning of salt and pepper. Form into 24 balls, cubes or egg shapes.

To make the sauce, thinly slice the onions and put in a

Curried Beef with Tropical Fruit

large roasting dish. Stir in the oil and, without covering, cook, stirring occasionally until the onions brown (about 12 minutes). Stir in the remaining sauce ingredients and, without covering, cook until the mixture is boiling (about 5 minutes). Purée in a liquidizer and pour back into the roasting dish.

Add the meat balls, gently stirring and turning them so that all are coated with the sauce. Cover and vent and cook, stirring occasionally, until the meat balls are just tender (about 5 minutes). Cover and set aside.

To prepare the fruit garnish, peel the pineapple, cutting the flesh into 2 cm/¾ inch cubes. Peel the mango over a bowl and slice into strips, reserving any juice. Rinse the kumquats. In a large bowl, blend the fruit juices and the mango chutney. Stir in the fruit. Cover and cook until the pineapple is slightly soft (about 3 minutes). Stir in the kumquats and cook until they are hot and just softening (about 1 minute). Keep covered.

Blend the yogurt and cornflour together. Stir into the meat and, without covering, cook, stirring once, until bubbling (about 2 minutes).

Pour the meat balls and sauce into the centre of a heated shallow platter and surround with a border of the cooked fruit.

VEAL PÉRIGOURD

It is important not to overcook the escalopes which it is very easy to do since they are so thin. Cooking can be judged by change of colour and also texture which, if overcooked, will appear dry and the meat will tend to curl up.

SERVES 4 to 6

◆

4-6 × 70 g/2½ oz veal escalopes
170 g/6 oz button mushrooms
2 tablespoons flour
Salt and white pepper
30 g/1 oz butter
140 ml/¼ pint double cream
2 tablespoons brandy
Garnish
1 or 2 raw broccoli florets, finely chopped

◆

Flatten the escalopes with a cleaver or rolling pin between two pieces of cling film – this prevents the meat from flaking. Finely slice the mushrooms. Spread the flour on cling film and season with salt and pepper. Coat both sides of the escalopes with the flour.

Put the butter in a large shallow dish. Cover and cook on Full Power until bubbling (about 45 seconds). Immediately uncover and lay the veal escalopes in the butter in a single layer. Without covering, cook until the end and side pieces are opaque (about 1 minute). Turn the escalopes over, at the same time repositioning them so that those in the centre are on the outside. Toss in any remaining flour. Reduce the setting to Defrost (35%) and cook until all the meat is opaque (about 1½ minutes). Transfer the veal to a warm flameproof dish.

Stir the mushrooms into the juices remaining in the dish. Cover, raise the setting to Full Power and cook, stirring once, until tender (about 3 minutes). Stir in the cream. Reduce the setting to Defrost (35%) and without covering, cook, stirring occasionally, to reheat (about 2 minutes). If necessary, replace the veal in the sauce and, without covering, reheat on Defrost (35%) (about 1 minute). Transfer the veal and sauce to the hot flameproof dish.

Put the brandy in a mug and, without covering, heat on Full Power for 15-20 seconds. Immediately pour over the veal and ignite with a taper. When the flames have died down, garnish with the chopped broccoli.

PORK STROGANOFF

Traditionally Stroganoff is served with boiled rice. It is very rich and a crisp side salad is a good accompaniment.

SERVES 5 to 6

680 g/1½ lb lean pork (weight after trimming)
2 tablespoons dry red wine
2 tablespoons salad oil
30 g/1 oz butter
1 onion
340 g/12 oz button mushrooms
1 tablespoon French mustard
Salt and freshly milled black pepper
140 ml/¼ pint soured cream
2 teaspoons cornflour

Prick the pork deeply all over, then cut into 4 cm × 5 mm/1½ × ¼ inch strips. Combine the wine and oil in a large bowl and add the pork strips, stirring to completely coat. Leave for 2-4 hours, stirring occasionally. Put the butter in a large casserole and, without covering, heat on Full Power until melted (about 30 seconds).

Finely chop the onion and stir into the butter. Without covering, cook on Full Power until just tinged with gold. Quarter the mushrooms, stir into the softened onion, cover and cook on Full Power for 4 minutes. Stir in the mustard and add salt and pepper to taste. Mix in the pork strips and marinade, cover and cook on Full Power to initially heat the meat (about 3 minutes). Stir. Reduce the setting to Defrost (35%), cover and cook, stirring occasionally, until the pork is cooked through (about 12 minutes). Blend the soured cream and cornflour together. Stir into the pork and, without covering, cook on Defrost (35%), stirring occasionally, until the mixture thickens (about 5 minutes). Serve hot.

Note: If preparing in advance, only add the soured cream thickening when reheating. Extra time will be needed to heat the dish from cold.

CHICKEN IN CLAM SAUCE

Canned baby clams are only available at specialist delicatessens, but it is well worth tracking them down.

SERVES 6

1 × 1.6 - 1.8 kg/3½-4 lb chicken, or 6 partly-boned chicken breasts
1 small onion
1 stick celery
1 clove garlic
1 × 190 g/6¾ oz can pimientos
1 teaspoon dried tarragon
15 g/½ oz butter
1 tablespoon olive oil
1 × 400 g/14 oz can chopped tomatoes
5 tablespoons tomato purée
140 ml/¼ pint water
Salt and freshly milled black pepper
1 × 285 g/10 oz can baby clams
1 tablespoon freshly chopped parsley

Skin and cut the whole chicken into six pieces or skin the chicken breasts. Peel and quarter the onion. Scrape and cut up the celery. Peel the garlic. Drain and roughly chop the pimientos.

Chop the onion, celery and garlic together in a food processor, then spoon into a large casserole. Add the tarragon, butter and oil. Cover and cook on Full Power, stirring occasionally, until the vegetables are tender (about 6 minutes). Stir in the chopped pimientos, the tomatoes and their juice, tomato purée and water. Without covering, cook, stirring occasionally, until reduced by one-third (about 15 minutes). Mash with a fork. Season to taste. Add the chicken pieces. Cover and cook until the chicken is nearly tender, turning and repositioning the portions once during cooking (about 20 minutes). Cover and leave to stand for 20 minutes.

Mix the clams into the casserole. Reduce the setting to Defrost (35%), cover and reheat until hot (about 10 minutes). Stir in parsley and serve at once.

Note: Provided the casserole is rapidly cooled, it can be stored in the refrigerator or the freezer to be thawed and reheated when required. Commence thawing on Full Power (about 10 minutes), then reposition the pieces. Reduce the setting to Defrost (35%) and continue cooking until thoroughly hot (30-45 minutes).

FILETS DE DINDE AU JARDIN VERT

Thinly-sliced turkey fillets are served on a bed of green vegetables flavoured with Emmenthal and lime and accompanied by a sauce made of ground almonds, white wine and parlsey. You need only serve a garnish of sautéed potatoes to accompany this filling dish.

SERVES 6

◆

6 skinned turkey breasts (about 680 g/1½ lb total weight)
2 large green peppers
1 clove garlic
1 medium onion
1 large courgette
4 dark green cabbage leaves
2 tablespoons Emmenthal cheese
1 tablespoon olive oil
115 g/4 oz green beans, sliced
170 g/6 oz mange-tout
1 tablespoon tomato purée
1 teaspoon dried marjoram
1 teaspoon dried sage leaves
2 limes
Salt and freshly milled black pepper
1 tablespoon ground almonds
4 tablespoons dry white wine
1 tablespoon arrowroot
30 g/1 oz finely chopped parsley

◆

Slice or butterfly the turkey fillets. Core, seed and slice the peppers into rings. Peel and crush the garlic. Slice the onion. Top, tail and slice the courgette. De-vein, roll and finely slice the cabbage. Grate the cheese.

Mix the oil, peppers, garlic and onion in a large casserole. Cover and cook on Full Power until the vegetables soften, stirring once or twice during cooking (about 8 minutes). Add the courgette, cabbage, green beans, mange-tout, tomato purée, marjoram, sage and cheese and a squeeze of lime juice. Mix together thoroughly. Cover and cook until all the vegetables are tender, stirring twice during cooking (about 12 minutes). Squeeze the juice of half a lime over the turkey breasts and place them on top of the vegetables. Season to taste with salt and pepper. Cover and cook for about 6 minutes. Reposition and turn the turkey slices over. Cover and continue cooking until they are tender (about 6 minutes).

To prepare the sauce, mix the ground almonds, wine and arrowroot in a small bowl with 6 tablespoons of the cooking liquid from the turkey and vegetables. Mix in the parsley and season to taste. Without covering, cook on Full Power, stirring occasionally, until the sauce thickens (about 1½ minutes). Meanwhile, slice the remaining lime. Spoon the sauce over the turkey breasts and garnish with the lime slices.

POULET MARIE HÉLÈNE

Stuffed chicken breasts are masked with a saffron sauce. To save time, both the filling and the infused milk can be prepared ahead. Allow extra time if the ingredients have been refrigerated. The entire dish may be prepared in advance and stored in a cool place. Reheat, covered, on the Defrost (35%) setting.

SERVES 6

❖

285 ml/½ pint milk
10 strands saffron
1 clove garlic
6 × 115-170 g/4-6 oz chicken breasts, skinned
115 g/4 oz chicken livers
2 lean rashers bacon
2-3 sage leaves
1 × 285 g/10 oz can creamed sweetcorn
Salt and freshly milled black pepper
30 g/1 oz butter
20 g/¾ oz flour
Garnish
Sage leaves

❖

Put the milk, saffron strands and peeled garlic in a jug and heat on Full Power until 1 or 2 bubbles appear around the edges (about 3½ minutes). Cover and set aside, stirring occasionally (about 30 minutes).

Meanwhile, flatten the chicken breasts between two pieces of cling film, using a rolling pin or cleaver.

Trim, rinse and finely chop the livers. De-rind and chop the bacon. Finely cut the sage leaves with scissors. Mix the livers, bacon and herbs together in a bowl. Cover and cook, stirring occasionally, until the livers are opaque (about 3 minutes). Purée in a liquidizer with the sweetcorn. Season to taste, using salt sparingly.

Divide the mixture and place a spoonful in the centre of each chicken breast. Fold the chicken into parcels, tucking in the sides to ensure that the filling is completely enclosed. Arrange seam-side down in a single layer in a large shallow dish. Cover and cook until the outside parcels change colour (about 5 minutes). Turn the parcels over and reposition, placing those that are less well done towards the outside. Cover and cook until done on all sides (about 5 minutes). Pink patches showing underneath indicate insufficient cooking; a shrivelled white appearance is a sign of overcooking. If necessary, remove each parcel as soon as it is ready, transferring it to a warm serving dish. Keep covered.

To complete the sauce, stir the butter into the hot juices remaining in the dish and mix in the flour. Strain in the flavoured milk and stir with a whisk. Without covering, cook, whisking three times during cooking, until the sauce thickens (about 3 minutes). Season to taste.

Pour the sauce over the hot chicken parcels and serve at once. If made of suitable material for the microwave, reheat the entire dish on the Defrost (35%) setting (about 3 minutes) before serving.

CHICKEN AND PRAWN RISOTTO

This basic risotto can be varied to suit all tastes. Tarragon imparts a delicate flavour but thyme, oregano or wild marjoram can be substituted. Tuna or salmon may take the place of prawns.

SERVES 5 to 6

❖

225 g/8 oz skinned and boned raw chicken or turkey
30 g/1 oz butter or margarine
170 g/6 oz easy cook long grain rice
115 g/4 oz cooked or frozen cut green beans
170 g/6 oz shelled cooked prawns
1½ teaspoons freshly chopped or ½ teaspoon dried tarragon
425 ml/¾ pint hot water
Salt and pepper
Whole cooked prawns to garnish

❖

Cut the chicken into small bite-sized pieces. Put the butter or margarine in a 2 litre/3½ pint casserole and, without covering, heat on Full Power until melted (about 45 seconds). Stir in the rice and cook without covering, stirring once, until all the grains are evenly coated (about 1½ minutes). Stir in the remaining ingredients, adding salt and pepper to taste.

Cover and cook on Full Power for about 10 minutes. Stir, recover and cook until the liquid is nearly absorbed and the rice grains almost cooked (about 7 minutes). Stir quickly but thoroughly, then immediately replace the lid and leave to stand for 5 to 7 minutes before serving.

Garnish each portion with whole prawns and serve with creamed sweetcorn and a green salad.

CHOCOLATE CHERRY LOG WITH HOT CHERRY MOCHA SAUCE

Carob powder, although similar to chocolate in flavour and colour, is very much lighter in texture, and when used in baking, the results are softer. If you have no suitably-shaped container, such as the lid of a glass chicken roaster, make a box from a large sheet of non-stick baking parchment.

SERVES 6

❖

3 large eggs
85 g/3 oz caster sugar
30 g/1 oz carob powder, sifted
30 g/1 oz wholemeal flour
1 tablespoon farina (potato flour)
1 tablespoon hot water
285 ml/½ pint double cream
1 teaspoon Kirsch
1 × 425 g/15 oz can black cherries
2 tablespoons grated chocolate
Sauce
140 ml/¼ pint juice from the cherries
About 4 tablespoons milk
15 g/½ oz carob powder
1 teaspoon vanilla essence
¼ teaspoon coffee granules
1 tablespoon arrowroot
30 g/1 oz butter
1-2 tablespoons caster sugar

❖

Lightly grease a 25 × 15 cm/10 × 6 inch shallow rectangular dish. Line the base with non-stick baking parchment.

Separate the eggs and put the yolks in a mixing bowl. Whisk with an electric beater until frothy. Add the 85 g/3 oz of caster sugar and continue whisking until thick and the consistency of soft ice cream. Fold in the carob and flours, sprinkle with the water and fold in. Using clean beaters in a grease-free bowl, whisk the egg whites to stiff peaks. Fold into the cake mixture in three batches. Pour into the lined dish. Without covering, cook on Full Power until just dry on top (about 3½ minutes). The edges may remain slightly moist. Leave to stand for 5 minutes.

Lift the parchment and cake onto a work surface and roll up from one narrow end so that the 'swiss roll' is fully lined. Leave to cool. Whip the cream and Kirsch together until thick. Drain the cherries, reserving the juice and fold into the cream. Carefully unroll the cake and gently remove the parchment lining. Spread with the cream, cherries and chocolate and reroll without pressure, which would cause the filling to ooze. Trim the ends with a sharp knife. Cover loosely and keep cool.

To make the sauce, measure the cherry juice and if necessary make up to 140 ml/¼ pint with milk. Mix in a medium bowl with the milk, carob powder, vanilla essence, coffee granules and arrowroot. Add the butter. Without covering, cook on Full Power, stirring frequently with a whisk, until the sauce thickens (about 3 minutes).

Serve the cake in thick slices with a spoonful of the hot sauce.

MELON AND GINGER MERINGUE

This is a unique microwave recipe in which the fruit remains raw while the meringue cooks to a mallow-like texture. To achieve the best results, chill the melon balls before covering with the meringue. Choose ripe yet firm-fleshed melons and, if preferred, one large honeydew can be substituted for two smaller fruit. The honeydew melons are usually cheaper than the other varieties. The ogen and galia melons have green flesh and the cantaloupe and charentais are an orangey colour. It is interesting to combine them to produce a variety of colours and flavours.

SERVES 4

❖

**2 small melons
115 g/4 oz crystallized ginger
4 egg whites
115 g/4 oz caster sugar
½ teaspoon ground ginger
2 tablespoons chopped pistachios**

❖

Halve the melons through the stalk ends and discard the seeds. Using a potato baller or teaspoon, scoop out marble-sized pieces of flesh, leaving a firm wall. Put the melon balls in a colander over a bowl and cover with the upturned melon shells. Leave until well drained.

Slice the ginger, mix with the melon balls and pile into the shells. Whisk the egg whites until stiff, then gradually whisk in the sugar to form a stiff meringue. Sprinkle with the ground ginger and fold in with a metal spoon. Spoon the meringue over the fruit, making sure it reaches the edges. Without covering, cook two melon halves at a time on Full Power, giving each a half turn halfway through cooking until the meringue puffs up considerably (about 3½ minutes). Scatter with the chopped pistachios and serve immediately. Use the reserved melon juice to mix with other fruit juices and serve as a cold drink.
Note: You will get an even better result if you brown the meringue topping under the grill.

While the melons are cooking, prepare a hot grill, placing the rack at least 15 cm/6 inches from the element or flame. Place the melon halves on a tray and brown briefly under the grill (about 10 seconds). The meringue burns quickly, so it must be watched constantly. Serve as soon as possible. When cold, the meringue tends to sink but the flavour is unimpaired.

PEACH BRULÉE

Substitute apricots for nectarines if peaches are difficult to obtain. Well-drained, sliced fruit in natural juice can also be used, but avoid fruits that soften or discolour, such as bananas or pears. When making the syrup, take extreme care as syrups darken and burn quite suddenly. It is better to err on the safe side, watching carefully towards the end of cooking. The cooking container must be heatproof and care should be taken when removing it from the microwave.

SERVES 6

❖

**3 firm peaches
6 egg yolks
425 ml/¾ pint double cream
1½ teaspoons cornflour
4 tablespoons caster sugar
Caramel
12 tablespoons caster sugar
12 tablespoons water**

❖

Halve, stone and skin the peaches. Thinly slice and arrange in the base of a heatproof serving dish.

Lightly beat the egg yolks and cream together and strain into a large bowl. Thoroughly stir in the cornflour and sugar with a wire whisk. Without covering cook on Full Power, stirring every minute, until hot (about 3 minutes). Continue cooking, stirring every 30 seconds, until the sauce is thickened to the consistency of half-whipped cream (about 3½ minutes). Should you notice curdling beginning around the edges, beat vigorously for 1 minute. Pour the thickened custard on to the fruit, then chill until firm. Freeze for 30 minutes or until absolutely hard.

To make the caramel topping, mix the sugar and water in a 1·2 litre/2 pint ovenproof glass jug or bowl. Without covering, cook until hot (about 2 minutes). Stir until the sugar has dissolved. Continue cooking until the syrup is dark golden but not brown (about 15-20 minutes). Immediately remove from the microwave using oven gloves. Leave for 2 minutes until the colour darkens, then pour a thin layer over the chilled custard. Leave until the caramel is set and brittle and the filling thaws.

WHITE DINNER MINTS

These mints can be stored for several weeks in the refrigerator and as white rather than dark chocolate is used no bloom occurs to spoil the appearance.

SERVES 16

◆

115 g/4 oz white chocolate
15 g/½ oz butter
1 tablespoon Crème de Menthe
1 tablespoon cocoa powder
55 g/2 oz icing sugar, sifted

◆

Break up the chocolate and put half in a small bowl or jug. Without covering, heat on Full Power until just shiny on top (about 1 minute). Stir until melted. Pour onto a sheet of greaseproof or non-stick paper and spread to a 12.5 cm/5 inch square. Leave in a cool place until firm. Put the remaining chocolate in the same bowl or jug and set aside.

Put the butter in a medium bowl and heat until melted (about 30 seconds). Add the Crème de Menthe and gradually work in the cocoa and sugar to form a smooth paste. Using a round-bladed knife, spread evenly over the chocolate square. Leave until beginning to set.

Melt the remaining chocolate (about 1 minute). Pour over the mint mixture so that it is completely covered. Leave until set. Using a sharp, slightly warmed knife, trim the edges and cut into squares.

Chocolate Cherry Log with Hot Mocha Sauce (*see page 92*) and White Dinner Mints

OLD ENGLISH SHERRY TRIFLE

Use an attractive utensil, such as a glass or non-metal trimmed soufflé dish, to cook the cake base. Add the remaining ingredients and serve directly from this dish. Alternatively, cook the cake base separately in any microwave-suitable cake container and transfer to your chosen serving dish.

SERVES 6 to 8

❖

Cake base
55 g/2 oz butter
30 g/1 oz white cooking fat
85 g/3 oz caster sugar
1 egg, beaten
3 tablespoons warm milk
115 g/4 oz self-raising flour
Topping
140 ml/¼ pint medium sherry
3 tablespoons raspberry jam
170 g/6 oz raspberries, fresh or frozen
Custard
285 ml/½ pint milk
½-1 teaspoon vanilla essence
2 eggs
1 tablespoon caster sugar
To decorate
285 ml/½ pint whipping cream
Glacé cherries and chopped angelica

❖

To make the cake, beat the butter, cooking fat and sugar together until light and fluffy. Stir the egg and milk together and gradually beat into the mixture. Fold in the flour thoroughly. Spoon into a deep, 15 cm/6 inch round glass or plastic cake dish. Without covering, cook on Full Power until the mixture is only just dry on top (about 3½ minutes).

Turn out and transfer to a similar sized bowl or leave in the baking container. Pour the sherry evenly over the cake and cut roughly into squares to enable the sherry to thoroughly penetrate. Spread with the jam and cover with the raspberries.

To make the custard, beat together the milk, vanilla essence, eggs and sugar in a medium bowl. Without covering, cook, beating every 30 seconds, until the sauce thickens around the edges (about 3 minutes). Continue cooking, beating every 15 seconds, until the sauce is creamy and mousse-like (about 1 minute). Do not overcook or the sauce will curdle. Signs of curdling first appear around the edges and if this occurs beat vigorously for several minutes. Pour over the cake mixture, cover and leave to cool in the refrigerator.

Whip the cream to soft peaks and spread over the set custard. Decorate with quartered glacé cherries and chopped angelica.

RASPBERRY AND REDCURRANT SORBET

This is a glorious deep pink, creamy sorbet that needs no added colouring or flavouring. A tight-budded rose together with one or two leaves shows this off to advantage.

SERVES 6

❖

170 g/6 oz caster sugar
200 ml/7 fl oz water
340 g/12 oz redcurrants, untrimmed
170 g/6 oz raspberries
To decorate
Raspberries and redcurrants
A freshly picked rose and its leaves (optional)

❖

Stir together the sugar and water in a large bowl. Without covering, cook on Full Power until hot (about 3 minutes). Stir until the sugar has dissolved, then heat until boiling and continue cooking until a thin syrup is formed (about 8 minutes). Put the untrimmed redcurrants and the raspberries in a large bowl. Without covering, cook until the skins are soft (about 7 minutes). Put through a sieve into the bowl of syrup, pressing with a wooden spoon until only the pips and stalks remain. Discard these. Thoroughly mix the syrup and fruit purée. Without covering, freeze until partly frozen (about 2 hours). Beat thoroughly with an electric whisk or purée in a liquidizer, then refreeze until required.

Remove from the freezer 10 minutes before serving and use an ice cream scoop that has been dipped in cold water to obtain well-rounded shapes. Decorate each serving with a few fresh raspberries and redcurrants and place a rose on the side of the plate, if liked.

ORANGE AND LEMON SOUFFLÉ

SERVES 8

❖

4 large eggs
1 orange
1 lemon
85 g/3 oz caster sugar
1 tablespoon powdered gelatine
285 ml/½ pint double cream
To decorate
Rosettes of whipped cream and Mimosa balls

❖

Separate the eggs. Squeeze the juice and grate the rind from the orange and lemon. Mix 6 tablespoons of fruit juice, all the rind and the sugar in a medium bowl. Without covering, cook on Full Power until hot (about 1½ minutes). Stir until the sugar dissolves, then continue cooking until fast boiling (about 1 minute). Remove the bowl from the microwave, beat the egg yolks and strain into the syrup from a height, beating vigorously preferably with an electric beater.

Put 4 tablespoons of water in a mug and stir in the gelatine. Without covering, cook until very hot (about 1½ minutes). Stir until dissolved. Pour the dissolved gelatine into the syrup, holding the mug about 15 cm/6 inches above the bowl, and beat vigorously. Leave until cold but not set. Half-whip the cream to soft peaks and fold into the lightly-jellied mixture. Using clean beaters, whisk the egg whites to stiff peaks. Stir 1 tablespoon of the egg whites into the cream, then fold in the remainder using a large metal spoon.

Cut a double thickness of greaseproof paper one and a half times the circumference and the height of the dish plus 2.5 cm/1 inch. Wrap around the outside of the dish and secure with string or a large rubber band. Make sure there is no gap between the collar and the sides of the dish. Pour the soufflé mixture into the dish, allowing it to rise above the edge of the dish but not beyond the edge of the greaseproof paper. Leave to set. Refrigerate or freeze until required.

Before serving, remove the collar. Cut away the string or rubber band and slide a warmed round-bladed knife between the paper collar and the edges of the soufflé. Decorate the top with rosettes of whipped cream and Mimosa balls.

CHOCOLATE NESTS SABAYON

SERVES 4 to 8

❖

115 g/4 oz dark dessert chocolate
¼ teaspoon salad oil
135 g/4¾ oz lime-flavoured table jelly
1 egg
1 egg yolk
2 tablespoons caster sugar
115 g/4 oz white milk chocolate
3 tablespoons sherry
1 × 213 ml/7½ fl oz carton UHT double cream

❖

Break up the dark dessert chocolate and put into a small bowl. Without covering, heat on Full Power until shiny and beginning to melt (about 2 minutes), then stir in the oil. Pour 1 teaspoon of melted chocolate into each mould and swirl or brush to coat thinly. Leave in a cool place until set. Coat with a second spoon of chocolate in the same way. Add a third coat if necessary. Before turning out, put in the freezer for up to 15 minutes. This helps to shrink the moulds away from the chocolate. Invert the moulds onto greaseproof paper, press round the edges with the fingers, then smartly tap the open end of the mould on the paper. The eggs will release easily. Treat the moulds again before preparing the next batch.

To make the jelly, put 140 ml/¼ pint of cold water in a jug. Add the jelly cubes and, without covering, cook until very hot but not boiling (about 3 minutes). Stir until dissolved. Add cold water to make up to 425 ml/¾ pint, then stir to blend thoroughly. Pour into a clean 33 × 23 cm/13 × 9 inch baking tray and refrigerate until set.

To make the filling, use an electric beater to whisk the whole egg and egg yolk until fluffy. Add the sugar and continue beating until thick. Break up the white chocolate and put into a jug or basin with the sherry. Without covering, heat until the chocolate is beginning to melt and the sherry is hot (about 2 minutes). Stir to mix. Pour into the mousse and beat vigorously until very thick. Add the cream and continue beating until the mousse is thick once more. Refrigerate until cold.

Fill the chocolate shell halves with the mousse and refrigerate or freeze until required. Chop the jelly with a damp, round-bladed knife. Allow two or three chocolate shell halves per person and arrange on a large platter or individual plates surrounded by a bed of chopped jelly.

Microwaves cook by the rubbing together of molecules of water, fats and sugar in food and drink. As this friction becomes more vigorous, the food naturally becomes hotter and, whether defrosting, reheating or cooking, the microwave process is the same. When cooking in a conventional oven, the outside layer of food heats first and at the highest temperature; the remaining layers of food heat by conduction from this outer one. The dry heat in the conventional oven, whether a radiant heat or convection heat which operates by use of a fan, dries and seals and browns the outer layer. For this reason, foods that need to remain soft, such as a casserole, are cooked covered. In microwave cookery, the outer 2.5-4 cm/ 1-1½ inches cooks simultaneously and the food nearer the centre is cooked by weaker microwave signals and by conduction from the outer layers in a similar way to the conventional method. Foods cooked by microwave will not crispen on the outside. They will either crispen throughout or will remain soft throughout.

In the conventional oven, cooking times are influenced by the bulk or size of the food rather than by the number of items being baked simultaneously. For example, a joint of meat is cooked according to its weight, but ten fairy cakes will take the same length of time as sixty fairy cakes. In the microwave oven, both the quantity and the composition of that food determines the length of cooking time. The power output on the microwave affects the speed of cooking as does composition, size and shape of containers.

MICROWAVE
TECHNIQUES

Always use the microwave for all those tedious little jobs that you would normally have to get a bowl or saucepan out for – for example, melting chocolate. It is a simple matter to break up the chocolate, place it in a jug and, without covering, heat on Full Power until the surface is just shiny. The chocolate will then finish dissolving as it is thoroughly stirred.

Sprinkle gelatine into a few tablespoons of water, bring to the boil and stir thoroughly until dissolved.

To dry herbs, remove the stalks and place the leaves between two sheets of kitchen paper. Heat on Full Power, stirring frequently with the fingers, until the leaves are nearly dry. Remove from the microwave and leave to stand at room temperature whereupon the drying will complete without further cooking.

Warm baby foods in the open jars on the Defrost level, stirring frequently, and babies' bottles with the teats removed can also be warmed on the Defrost control. However, take very great care that you shake the bottle thoroughly to mix the hot parts with the cold parts after you have fixed the teat in position. Otherwise, the baby's mouth could be burned.

Although it is possible to use the microwave for all sorts of softening or warming jobs, there is one that you must never attempt and that is to dry out newspapers or tea cloths, because the dried-out parts would catch on fire.

The microwave is a long-lasting, dependable and well built machine which should give you many years of satisfaction by simplifying food preparation and helping you to run your kitchen more efficiently.

HOW THE MICROWAVE WORKS

Microwaves are a form of electro-magnetic energy which is similar to that used for transmitting radio and television. These waves are invisible and travel at the speed of light. When the microwave is switched on and the oven is ready for use, the magnetron (the main component) converts electricity into microwaves. The waves then enter the cavity via a wave channel to make them more efficient as they must be broken up. Various methods are used for this, including a stirrer fan, either in the ceiling or underneath the oven floor, a turntable, or some other device. The microwaves reach the metal linings which prevent them from passing out of the oven and so change direction, but find the metal once again blocking their passage. They are, in fact, trapped and so become agitated. Additionally, the microwaves do not like being broken up and constantly struggle to realign themselves. In their attempts to do this they create enormous movement in the food particles, tossing them about violently. As a result of this friction, heat is created and defrosting, reheating and cooking take place.

Microwaves cannot escape from the oven because the door when closed is totally sealed and the window mesh is too fine for the microwaves to pass through. The action cuts out when the door is opened.

UTENSILS TO USE IN THE MICROWAVE

Bakeware and cooking utensils should not impede the microwaves as they try to get into and through the food. It is, therefore, essential to choose containers made of suitable materials – these include glass, glass ceramics, stoneware, pottery, some plastics, wood and paper.

Ovenglass bowls, casseroles and pie plates that you may have collected or inherited over the years all come into their own for microwave cooking. They allow the microwaves to pass through without affecting their efficiency. The dishes remain extremely cool and easy to handle.

Corning white microwave ware and vision pans are top of the list because their resistance to exceedingly high temperatures enables them to go from the freezer to the microwave, to the hob, the conventional oven or under the grill, and still look good enough to serve from.

Ordinary glass is microwave suitable provided it can withstand the heat transmitted from the food. Very thick or very thin glass could crack, particularly if a hairline crack already exists. Crystal is definitely *not* suitable. It has a lead content and when placed in the microwave would explode. Crystal has even been known to explode after removal from the microwave, causing serious injuries. Needless to say, do not reheat a dessert in such a bowl.

Unglazed earthenware, which is the material used for making the famous cooking bricks, absorbs moisture and is normally soaked before use. It will heat up during microwaving and become almost too hot to handle. However, one advantage is that it slows down cooking times and is therefore a better dish to use when cooking meat casseroles.

Clay flower pots make ideal vessels for cake or bread-making. A chocolate cake made in a newly-purchased plant pot can be decorated with marzipan leaves and flowers to give a realistic appearance.

Ironstone is unsuitable for microwaving as it has metal particles in its composition.

China, provided it has no decoration and is not antique, is attractive to use for short cooking times when food is to be served directly from it.

There is a vast family of plastics, most of which are satisfactory for use in microwaves – the type of food will govern your choice. Generally speaking it is best to use those that are sold specifically for microwave use. Some plastics, for example the kind that yogurt pots are made of, will quickly collapse in the microwave. They will similarly distort if boiling water is poured into them, as they are not resistant to high temperatures. If plastic containers are dishwasher proof, then they will be resistant to temperatures up to 85°C/180°F and so can be used for warming only.

The type of food being heated will have considerable effect on what containers can be used. Fats, sugars and syrups quickly reach very high temperatures, so it would be unwise to heat or cook a syrup sponge pudding in a plastic container. Polystyrene beakers are adequate for heating drinks, but do not use the flat, foam dishes (the kind that are used for packaging in supermarkets) for cooking. Fats will melt the plastic and, if covered, the trapped steam will cause distortion.

Durable plastic cups and plates, such as Melamine, should definitely not be used for microwaving, because they become very hot, they distort and can scorch.

Specially-manufactured plastic dishes labelled continuous usage are more rigid and some are resistant to conventional oven temperatures up to 200°C/400°F/Gas Mark 6, enabling them to be transferred from the microwave to a moderate conventional oven, or they can be used in a combination oven.

There is a range of paper plates purposely coated with polyester which are dual purpose and are suitable for the freezer, microwave and conventional oven when set at moderate temperatures. Paper ware has many microwave uses. Use paper plates for heating dry items; paper napkins will absorb moisture when rolls, pastry, etc. are being warmed on them. Kitchen paper will absorb fat from sausages or bacon and should be placed over, rather than under, the food, to avoid sticking. Do not use coloured napkins; coloured kitchen paper is all right, provided the decorated side does not touch the food.

Waxed paper is undesirable as the wax might melt. Greaseproof paper when used for covering, allows the food to cook without becoming unduly soft. It does, however, tend to stick to chicken and fish. Non-stick baking parchment is ideal when absorption is not required and it has a bonus in that it can be washed and reused.

Sorting the way through the plastic jungle is made even more complicated by the variety of plastic bags, some of which can and some of which cannot be recommended for use in the microwave. Thin plastic food bags are not suitable. Freezer bags can be used for initial thawing but may melt and harden if fat or steam is in contact with the plastic. Boil-in-the-bags are thicker and have a high density, so they can be used for cooking smelly foods. Roasting bags are made of differing substances and can mainly be used for roasting but are also ideal for vegetable cookery. These bags usually come with metal tags and these must not be used at any time in the microwave. Invest in a box of rubber bands sufficiently large to close yet leave a 1 cm/½ inch opening.

Cling film may not always be recommended, but it does perform a useful job when covering is required, since casseroles have lids, but bowls do not. Except when using a microwave oven fitted with an auto-sensor, cling film should be applied loosely, pulling back a corner to leave a gap for the steam to escape. Another practical covering is a plastic lid that has a swivel closure.

Before using dishes for the first time, other than those specially recommended for the microwave, carry out this simple test: put the empty dish in the microwave and switch on for 30 seconds. If the dish feels hot, do not use any dishes from that range. If it feels warm, it will be satisfactory for a short period (*not* short term use). If the dish is cool, it is made of microwave-suitable material.

Some cups have glued-on handles and microwaving will cause the glue to dissolve and the handle to fall off – a highly dangerous occurrence.

METAL IN THE MICROWAVE

Since microwaves are reflected by metal, there is no purpose in trying to use metal casseroles; the microwaves simply cannot penetrate to reach the food. Some casseroles may resemble ceramics but are enamelled over cast iron. Any food put in them would remain raw no matter how long you microwaved it.

Foil dishes should only be used with the blessing of the microwave oven manufacturer. I have found that if these dishes are shallow, no more than 2 cm/¾ inch deep, are packed with food and not covered by a metallic coated lid, and do not come into contact with the oven linings, all is well. The food will heat fairly quickly, although not as quickly as in a non-metal dish. Deeper dishes are unsuitable as the metal edges are nearer to the magnetron and the microwaves therefore have a reduced chance of entering the food.

Small pieces of foil, provided they are smoothly placed and overwrapped in grease-proof paper, are useful when overcooking is likely – for example, on poultry wing tips and legs, or where food is uneven in depth (such as the tail of a Dover Sole or plaice, or the bone end of a leg of lamb). Use of flimsy metal, such as butter papers, chocolate wrappers, plastic or paper-coated tags from polythene bags and gold or silver decorated dishes, is highly dangerous. Flashing and crackling will be apparent during cooking and this shorting will damage and decrease the life of the magnetron.

Ordinary oven thermometers must not be left in poultry or meat joints during microwaving. The mercury could well blow up and break the thermometer glass and cause damage to the oven. Microwave-suitable thermometers *can* be left in the meat while cooking. Metal skewers must be fully embedded in the food and should stay at a distance from the oven linings and also not touch one another or the oven sides.

SIZES AND SHAPES OF UTENSILS

Bakeware and utensils must not only be made of materials that are 'transparent' to microwaves, but they must also be selected carefully for their size and shape. It is unlikely that the same recipe cooked in differing dishes will be identical in either appearance or texture. As soon as a dish has been perfected, always use the same container when repeating the recipe. Oval dishes and round dishes are superior to square ones. Rectangular dishes are only suitable when food can be stirred. When cooked in a square or rectangular dish, food that cannot be stirred will overcook in the corners. Container depth also plays a significant part in electronic cooking: tall-sided dishes partly shield the microwaves, while shallow dishes allow a freer passage.

Microwaves penetrate evenly and strongly to a depth of 2.5 cm/1 inch and they do this from all angles. Food placed in a shallow dish will have a greater area of exposure and will, therefore, cook more quickly than when in a deep dish. It is not a good idea to use a shallow dish that is too large, particularly when defrosting and there are thick pieces present in a sauce. The sauce will seep to the edges and dry out very quickly. Use deep dishes whenever food is likely to boil up. Cakes will double in volume on rising, so choose bakeware accordingly, and cakes will also cook more evenly in a ring mould. Bowls are perfect shapes because of the narrow diameter of the base, the curve of the sides, and the lack of sharp corners.

Container shapes and materials certainly have their effect upon the completed dishes, but many other factors are equally involved.

COOKING TIMES

Cooking times can never be accurately predicted for a number of reasons. Firstly there is a 10 per cent tolerance allowed by the manufacturers, meaning that an oven with a stated 600-watt output could actually vary between 540 and 660 watts and a 650-watt oven could be between 585 and 715 watts.

Line voltage into your home fluctuates and the microwave may be slower at peak periods, for example, when most people are using electricity to cook their evening meal.

The shape and material that the dishes are made of also affects cooking times and the type, density or age of the food is another governing factor. Microwave timings are also influenced by weight and quantity. Ingredients that start off cold will take longer to heat, and the amount of moisture in the food again has its effect.

Cooking times are equally variable when cooking conventionally, but we are so accustomed to these usual methods that we do not need to be so precise in the instructions in such recipes.

POWER LEVELS

Power levels on different ovens may be similar, but manufacturers do vary in their description; reference must be made to the manufacturer's handbook. What is 'low' on one model may be a raised or reduced power level on another. Full Power or High refers to the strongest microwave power the appliance can provide. A microwave oven rated at 700 watts will cook more quickly on Full Power (High) than a 600-watt oven. Only minor timing adjustments are required between the 600- and the 650-watt or the 650- and 700-watt ovens. Nowadays, small microwaves are in vogue as they are very cheap but they can only be used for fairly small quantities and the maximum power is 500 watts. Twenty per cent more time will need to be allowed.

The Defrost level is somewhere between 180 and 220 watts and is calculated at 35 per cent of Full Power; sometimes this is indicated by a symbol, a number (3 or 4), a percentage, or by a labelled description. The Defrost setting can also be used for cooking – a bonus when food cannot be stirred, such as Shepherds Pie or Lasagne. Its gentle power enables the food to cook and heat through to the middle without over-cooking around the edges. If your oven has lower settings, you will find these useful for slower but more even defrosting of joints and poultry as these sometimes tend to become warm when thawing on Defrost which is, of course, undesirable.

As a guide, use Full Power for cooking foods that can be stirred. There are, however, some exceptions: dishes that are likely to curdle when prepared in a saucepan or in an overhot oven will curdle if cooked on Full Power. Switch to Defrost for gentler heating as you would lower the heat in conventional cooking.

HOT AND COLD SPOTS

Uneven cooking happens in most conventional ovens: the sides may be hotter than the back and the top hotter than the bottom. Heating in the microwave is equally patchy, but you can turn this to your advantage when cooking in small jugs or dishes.

Place them in the 'hotter spot' to speed the cooking.

If you want to test for hot spots, space out several similar cups or ramekins half-filled with cold water in the microwave and watch to see which boils first. You will find it fascinating to watch this when they are on a turntable, as the bubbles rise and fall during rotation. Do not leave the dish in the microwave after a full boil is reached or the air bubbles will pop and splatter.

STIRRING AND COVERING

Stirring during cooking enables the food to be mixed to an even temperature. In circumstances that preclude stirring it will help to either turn or reposition the dishes.

Always cover food you wish to remain moist as you would in the conventional oven. Plates are suitable for covering but they do not leave a space for steam to escape. Specially-designed lids can be used to cover bowls or plates on which you are heating food, and casserole lids are useful when the quantity of liquid is small. Insert a wooden cocktail stick between the lid and the dish to form the required gap. Cling film, provided it does not touch the food, is a good choice. This can be vented by pulling back one corner. Cling film is less suitable if frequent stirring is necessary as it cannot easily be repositioned. If the dishes are covered leaving a 2.5 cm/1 inch gap, a spoon can be inserted for stirring without disturbing the covering.

Greaseproof paper is a very good covering material as it prevents splattering but does not trap in the heat. It does, however, tend to stick. Non-stick baking parchment does not stick but will blow off unless wrapped around the dish to hold it in place. Kitchen paper is absorbent and acts as a steamer as it also absorbs fat, but it can catch on fire if it becomes too dry.

DEFROSTING, REHEATING AND COOKING

Defrosting, reheating and cooking are all the same process, taking various times. Microwaves heat by friction and the longer they are operating, the hotter the food will become.

Some foods can be defrosted on the maximum setting: the sides of a frozen block of stew for example can be prised off with a fork as parts become thawed. Choose a dish shape that will fit the food snugly when reheating. Stirring during thawing prevents the gravy from spreading to the sides of the dish and drying up. Thaw individual bowls of soup on Full Power, stirring as bubbles appear around the edges, then carry on cooking and stir again to ensure that the hot and cold sections are properly mixed. Foods that cannot be stirred should be thawed on the Defrost setting.

Two or three dishes can be reheated simultaneously, provided each is removed as it is ready. Some foods will heat more quickly due to their composition. As a rule, foods that are slow to cook are also slow to reheat, but strangely enough these stay hot the longest. It is often suggested that standing times are given after microwaving is completed to enable internal temperatures to even out. This is equally true with foods that are roasted conventionally. In microwave cooking, any foods with a high sugar content, such as syrups, dried fruit, etc., retain too much heat and immediate consumption would result in burning the mouth. Only a few moments standing time is needed – usually the length of time it takes to set the food on the table.

To reheat plates of food, arrange the items well inside the perimeter of the plate. Wetter ingredients will heat the quickest so it is a good idea to heat meat with its gravy or fish with its sauce. Two plates can be stacked provided they are separated by a plastic ring – an air space between the underside of the top plate and the top of the bottom plate is essential and the top plate should be covered. Try to place the plates so that identical foods are staggered. Less even reheating will be obtained if, for example, peas are above peas, meat above meat and potatoes above potatoes.

As previously stated, microwaves penetrate to a depth of about 2.5 cm/1 inch, so that, if the food is deeper than 5 cm/2 inches, the inside will cook more slowly and by one hot layer heating the next. Food spread out in a shallow dish will cook more quickly than if completely filling a deeper one, even though the capacity is the same.

Sometimes thick foods soften very quickly underneath and the reason for this is that more steam heat is trapped on the underside of the food where it touches the dish. Turn large joints and potatoes over once during cooking to overcome this.

BROWNING

Microwaves do not brown the surface. Any browning that takes place will be because the ingredients are beginning to burn – for example, sugar, which caramelizes in any form of intense heat, and fats, which burn at high temperatures – and with microwaves this will happen inside the food and not necessarily be visible externally.

In order to make food appear brown, it must be treated either before or after cooking. Dark ingredients will deepen the colours of puddings and cakes – for example, chocolate and ginger seasonings, and spices such as turmeric and paprika, gravy browning, molasses and food colourings will all give a browned effect.

Frying is one of the usual methods of browning and this is not possible in the microwave. The fat temperature cannot be controlled so that deep-frying would be highly dangerous. Also condensation would cause droplets of moisture to drip back onto the hot fat and cause splattering. Shallow-frying or sautéeing in its truest sense, depends on the fat sealing and browning the exterior of the food. In point of fact, microwaves enter both the food and the fat simultaneously which is not really frying – I call it micro-frying and I find it useful for making croûtons and simulating fried, breaded items, such as fish cakes, fish fingers and schnitzels.

Browning dishes are special platters or casseroles that have a thin tin oxide coating sealed in under the base. These dishes are preheated in the microwave while empty until the surface becomes as hot as a frying pan. The food is then placed on the hot surface which gives instant browning. Browning dishes do sometimes fail to give satisfaction – this is not the fault of the design, it is the fault of the user. Once the food has touched the dish, the dish loses some of its heat and ensuing microwaving will not deepen the colour, although the food will continue to cook in the usual way.

Food should not be cold or the dish will cool too rapidly to be effective. Warm chops and sausages slightly for, say, 20 seconds before heating the browning dish to the manufacturer's recommended time. Add a little fat or oil, which will sizzle if the dish is hot enough, then immediately place the food in the dish, pressing it down with a fish slice. Flip it over straightaway and then microwave for the required time.

Never rest a hot browning dish on a work surface that cannot withstand a hot frying pan. Browning dishes should be cleaned with a soft dish cloth or sponge moistened with a liquid paste cleanser of the type used for saucepans.

MICROWAVING BASIC FOODS: EGGS

Scrambled eggs Making scrambled eggs is probably the first step to take in microwave cooking and you are bound to be put off if you are unsuccessful. When cooking scrambled eggs in a frying pan or saucepan, there is immediate direct heat on the bottom of the pan so that the food touching it starts cooking at once. Unless the pan is well greased the mixture will stick – to prevent this and also to achieve a 'scrambled' effect, constant stirring is therefore important. If a non-stick pan is used, the lumps move around easily but are inclined to have some crisp surfaces. Eggs scrambled in the microwave will, however, remain quite soft and the cooking jug or bowl is easier to wash. Choose a cooking vessel with a narrow diameter for 2 or 3 eggs, and a medium bowl for larger numbers. Before starting to cook, beat the eggs thoroughly with a fork or whisk adding 1 tablespoon of milk or water for each egg. Season to taste with salt and pepper. Add a knob of butter but do not try to beat it in as it will melt during cooking. Put the container in the microwave and, without covering, cook on Full Power, stirring or beating each time a ring of thickened mixture shows itself around the edges. When the eggs are scrambled yet soft and still slightly moist, they are ready to serve. Do not overcook as the eggs continue to dry and become firmer during the short time that it takes to dish them up. Two eggs will take about 1½ minutes, 4 eggs about 3 minutes, and 6 eggs about 4 minutes. Serve plain or mixed with grated cheese, diced ham or prawns, flaked tuna or salmon, parsley or capers. Slimmers might enjoy scrambled egg with watercress leaves and cottage cheese. For a more substantial meal, pipe islands of duchesse potato in a flat spiral fashion and brown under the grill. Pile scrambled egg on top and garnish with a slice of softened tomato and perhaps a sprig of parsley.

Poached eggs Conventionally poached eggs are cooked in a shallow frying pan in boiling salted or acidulated water. Microwave poached eggs are cooked in a similar fashion, and there will be no difference between the texture and taste. Single eggs cook in a neat shape in cereal bowls and two bowls can be placed side by side if they will fit into the microwave. Four or more eggs can be poached in a large shallow dish but they are likely to spread into one another. To poach 1 egg, half fill a suitable cereal or similar bowl with water (150-300 ml/¼-½ pint). Add salt or a few drops of vinegar. Without covering, bring to the boil (about 2-3 minutes). Meanwhile, break the egg into a saucer or cup. When the water is boiling rapidly, stir in a circular fashion with a wooden spoon handle and slide the egg into the centre. Try to do this in the microwave to save heat loss and keep the whirlpool going. Cover with an upturned undecorated saucer and cook on Full Power until just set (about 25-50 seconds). It is quite all right to remove the saucer to inspect halfway through cooking. There is no need to prick the egg yolk prior to cooking as the time is so short and the egg is surrounded by plenty of boiling water. Take the bowl from the microwave and remove the egg with a slotted spoon. A few wisps of white may remain in the water. Two eggs cooked in separate bowls will obviously take longer, as will 4 eggs in a large shallow dish. Should you wish to cook 1 single egg after the next, there is no need to throw away the cooking water. You will find the second egg cooks more quickly. Serve poached eggs on toast, on a bed of spinach or masked with a Hollandaise sauce.

Baked eggs Microwave baked eggs are similar to poached eggs but the white is much firmer. There is no need to prick the yolks, provided the eggs are cooked on the Defrost setting. Each egg should be broken into a well-greased egg poaching dish, ramekin or cup. Cover each with suitable plastic film (cling film is perfect so long as it does not touch the surface of the egg). Space out the dishes if more than one is being cooked in the microwave and cook on Defrost (35%) until the egg white is partially cooked (about 1 minute per egg). Give each dish a half turn and reposition, then continue cooking, covered, on the Defrost setting until the yolk is just set (about 1 minute per egg). Remove each egg as it sets and leave covered for 30 seconds before serving.

For a family meal, bake eggs in the same dish as the vegetables. For example, cook a ratatouille adding chopped frankfurters, diced ham or prawns. Place in a shallow dish and make four indentations or wells. Break an egg into each, then cover the dish and heat on the Defrost setting until the eggs are cooked.

Boiled eggs Eggs cannot be boiled in the normal way in the microwave because any item encased in a skin or shell will burst due to the expansion of air and the steam produced inside – and it is dangerous to try. However, there is a method of boiling eggs in the microwave which is most successful and this involves the use of foil. Although no time is saved, it can be very convenient. Have ready a kettle of boiling water. Wrap each egg individually and completely in smooth foil. Place in a jug or bowl and pour over sufficient boiling water to completely cover the eggs. A small bowl or jug is suitable for a single egg, and a very large bowl would be required for cooking 12 eggs simultaneously. Half cover the top of the jug or bowl with cling film and cook on Full Power according to conventional boiling times. Soft-boiled eggs will take 4-5 minutes and hard-boiled eggs 12-15 minutes. The cooking times need not be increased in proportion to the number of eggs being cooked as the microwaves are only heating and boiling the water and they are unable to reach the eggs because they cannot penetrate through the metal foil wrapping. So the eggs are, in fact, being cooked conventionally yet in the microwave. Do not try to reheat a hard-boiled egg before or after shelling as it may explode in your face.

Omelettes I do not normally recommend cooking omelettes in the microwave as it is very difficult to get an even texture throughout. A 2-egg omelette can be cooked in a well-heated browning dish, but will, of course, take on the shape of the dish. Use a

12.5 cm/5 inch round browning dish for a 2-egg omelette and the larger square browning dishes for 4- to 6-egg omelettes. Make sure that the eggs are at room temperature before beginning, then beat the eggs with a little milk and season with salt and pepper in the usual way. Preheat the browning dish for about three-quarters the maximum recommended time and have ready a generous knob of butter. When the dish is hot, add the butter, swirling it round if possible, then immediately pour in the beaten eggs. Return the dish to the microwave and, without covering, cook until the mixture bubbles and thickens around the edges. Loosen with a palette knife, allowing the uncooked mixture to run down the sides, then continue cooking until the surface is still slightly liquid. Remove from the microwave, flip one half of the omelette over the other and slide onto a hot serving dish. Preheating the small dish takes about 3 minutes and a large dish about 4½ minutes. It will take about 45 seconds for 2 eggs to cook and 1½ minutes for 4 eggs.

Soufflé omelettes The largest soufflé omelette that is possible in the microwave uses 3 eggs and should be cooked in a 23 cm/9 inch round dish. Separate the eggs and beat the 3 yolks with 3 tablespoons of milk, ¼ teaspoon of salt and ¼ teaspoon of white pepper. Using clean, grease-free beaters, whisk the egg whites in another bowl to stiff peaks. Stir 1 tablespoon of the beaten whites into the yolk mixture, then fold in the remainder. Put 15 g/½ oz of butter in the dish and, without covering, cook on Full Power for 45 seconds or until melted. Swirl the butter round the dish so that the sides are completely coated. Pour the egg mixture into the dish, reduce the setting and cook on Defrost (35%) for about 1 minute. Quickly open the door and give the dish a quarter turn. Cook for a further minute, then turn the dish again and repeat once more. Continue cooking until the mixture is barely set (about 2 minutes). Carefully slide the omelette onto a flame-proof dish or plate, flip over one side to fold, then brown under a preheated grill.

SAUCES
It is well worth mastering the techniques of sauce making. If you have a white sauce, a brown sauce and a Hollandaise sauce in your repertoire, you will be able to add all manner of other sweet and savoury ingredients to produce delicious meals.

White sauces Practice making a white sauce first. Since the microwave never produces lumpy sauces, half the battle is won. When you cook a white sauce in a pan on the hob, the bottom layer of liquid heats immediately and as the flour is heavier than the milk, it drops instantly to the bottom, absorbing the milk and thickening in lumps. Constant stirring is necessary to achieve a reasonable sauce. An added problem is that the straight sides of a saucepan make it difficult to stir in the edges. When the sauce is cooked by microwave, there is no direct heat, so for the first half of the cooking time there is no need to stir at all. Stirring only becomes necessary when the liquid is hot enough to have any effect upon the flour. Even if the sauce is lumpy for 75 per cent of the cooking time, these lumps will still whisk out smoothly and silkily at the end of cooking. Use the same proportions of butter or margarine, flour and milk as normal. For a coating sauce, you will need 30 g/1 oz of butter, 30 g/1 oz of flour and 285 ml/½ pint of milk. Use more milk for a thinner sauce and less milk for a thicker one. Should weighing out not be your strong point, ensure that there is more butter than flour. Put the butter in a bowl that will be the right size for the finished sauce and, without covering, melt on Full Power – it is unlikely that this will ever take more than 1 minute. As soon as the butter is soft, stir with a wire whisk and you may find that you do not need to melt additionally. If the butter is overmelted, it tends to clarify around the edges and then splatter and separate, although this does not have much effect upon the finished flavour. Stir the flour into the melted butter until all the particles are incorporated, then cook until the mixture becomes puffy and looks a little dry – this will take no more than 20-30 seconds. Add the milk all at once and stir with a wire whisk. Lots of little lumps will be floating around in the milk, but do not worry about this. Start microwaving, without covering, and cook for about 2½ minutes for 570 ml/1 pint of sauce, 1 minute for 285 ml/½ pint of sauce and 30 seconds for 140 ml/ ¼ pint of sauce. Stir, then continue cooking, stirring every 30 seconds or each time a thickened band of sauce appears around the edges of the bowl. Sometimes this occurs to such an extent that there remains only one small well in the middle, but however many mistakes are made, the sauce is still bound to be a success. Beat thoroughly and continue cooking until the sauce has thickened, then beat for a further 30 seconds to make sure that all the lumps have disappeared. Season to taste, adding any ingredients suitable for your requirements. Cheese sauce is one of the most popular and grated cheese can be added towards the end of cooking. Parsley should be fresh and finely chopped for parsley sauce but sorrel sauce and chervil sauce are equally easy and give a more subtle flavour. Chopped hard-boiled eggs, flaked tuna or salmon, chopped cooked chicken, sweetcorn or peas added to a thick white sauce provide a supper dish when served on toast, or fillings for hot vol-au-vent cases.

A thin white sauce is the basis of many a superior soup. Cook carrots, mushrooms, spinach, courgettes or any suitable vegetable in the microwave, then purée with the white sauce, adding flavourings to taste. These sauces are greatly enhanced when enriched with an egg yolk, beaten with a little double cream.

A white sauce need not be savoury; I have evolved several recipes using sweet in-gredients. For example, melt chocolate in a white sauce, adding a teaspoon of coffee granules for a very fine mocha sauce, or sweeten with honey and chopped orange segments, stir in puréed strawberries or raspberries and a little sugar to sweeten, or mix in 1 or 2 tablespoons of maple syrup and some grated hazelnuts for a lovely maple syrup sauce.

Brown sauces To make a real Espagnole sauce, you should use a container that can resist very high temperatures. Pyrex is heat resistant but Corning white microwave ware or Pyrosil is even more so. You will need oven gloves and a dry heatproof work surface to rest the bowl on after cooking as the mixture becomes very hot during cooking. The sauce feezes well, so it is probably better to make a larger quantity at one time. You will need 4 tablespoons of salad oil, 4 level tablespoons of plain flour, 2 tablespoons of very finely chopped onion, 2 tablespoons of very finely chopped celery, 2 tablespoons of very finely chopped lean bacon, 2 tablespoons of grated carrot, 1 tablespoon of freshly chopped parsley, ½ teaspoon of bay leaf powder, 1 tablespoon of tomato purée, 4 tablespoons of medium red wine, 570 ml/1 pint of strong hot beef stock, salt and freshly milled black pepper. If you prefer, you can chop the vegetables and bacon in a food processor which saves the bother of mincing and chopping separately. To make the sauce, blend the oil and flour together in a deep 1.7 litre/3 pint heatproof bowl or pan. Without covering, cook on Full Power, stirring occasionally, until the flour starts to brown (about 5 minutes). If you see a patch of burnt flour, stir instantly to get an even colour. Immediately mix in the onion, celery and bacon and, without covering, cook for about 2 minutes. Add all the remaining ingredients, three-quarters cover the bowl or pan and cook, stirring occasionally through the gap, for about 8 minutes until the sauce thickens. Purée in a liquidizer, then strain through a sieve. This recipe makes about 570 ml/1 pint.

Vegetarians will prefer to omit the bacon and use a vegetable stock. Add 1 teaspoon of vegetable yeast extract to give colour.

Hollandaise sauce Any conventional Hollandaise recipe can be converted to microwave cooking. When making a Hollandaise sauce conventionally, you need a double saucepan. The eggs are beaten in the top half with the liquid and then the butter is added in small pieces towards the end. In the microwave it is the other way round: the butter is melted before the other ingredients are added. To make a Hollandaise sauce, you will need 115 g/4 oz of unsalted butter, 2 egg yolks, 1½ tablespoons of fresh lemon juice, 3 tablespoons of double cream, salt and pepper. To make the sauce, put the butter in a large bowl and without covering, heat on Full Power until melted (about 1 minute). Beat the egg yolks, lemon juice and cream together and strain into the melted butter. Without covering, cook, beating every 15 seconds, until the sauce thickens (about 1 minute). Season to taste with salt and pepper. Hollandaise sauce freezes well but should be thawed very gently on the Defrost setting, stirring as soon as the edges soften. Vary the flavour by using orange or grapefruit juice and add a pinch of mustard for extra bite. If you prefer a thicker sauce, an extra egg yolk can be added.

Soups Most soups can be cooked by microwave, the best being those based on a thin white sauce. Allow 450 g/1 lb of sieved, cooked vegetables to every 570 ml/1 pint of thin white sauce, adding suitable flavourings and seasonings. Reheat after mixing together and stir during reheating. Spinach, carrot, mushroom, celery, celeriac, cauliflower, cucumber and avocado are all good choices.

There are, of course, many other ways of preparing soups and one of these is to sauté vegetables in a little butter before adding the liquid, then when very soft the mixture is liquidized and subsequently thickened with a *beurre manié* (which is an equal volume of butter and flour blended together), a blend of cornflour with cold water, or even a few tablespoons of double cream.

Should the soup be left to stand, and indeed it improves with standing, you will find that you have to add more stock or water when reheating.

Vegetables As with all other forms of microwave cookery, there are techniques and rules to follow when cooking vegetables, but these are flexible – rigidly following the charts will not necessarily turn the vegetables out the way you like them. Some people prefer their vegetables to be *'al dente'*, while others like their vegetables soft. Although it is wonderful to have them cooked quickly, allowing an extra 2 or 3 minutes is surely worth while if they are going to turn out better. Microwaved vegetables retain more vitamins and keep their colour because of the fast cooking, but there is no doubt that textures are improved if more water is used – this is not to say that the vegetables should be swamped. However, the more liquid that is added the longer the cooking time will be.

Fresh vegetables are normally cooked on Full Power. Prepare the vegetables in the usual way but put parsnips, salsify and Jerusalem artichokes in cold water to which you have added a little lemon juice until all are ready for cooking, otherwise they tend to blacken. Cut the vegetables into even-sized pieces, although carrots can be left whole if you prefer. Put the vegetables in a bowl or casserole and add sufficient water to reach halfway up. If you skimp on the water, you may find that some of the vegetables, particularly the top layer, are spongy and this is an indication of drying out. Since it is healthier to eat less salt, it is better to salt the water rather than add it after cooking as it penetrates the food more this way. The salt must never be sprinkled onto the vegetables as this dries them out, particularly those parts of the vegetable that protrude above the water. Preferably use a deep oval casserole or choose a round casserole with a narrow diameter. Cover completely for the first half of the cooking time, then reposition or stir. In the case of whole carrots or large pieces, make sure that the lower ones that have been completely immersed in the water are then put on the top. During the second half of cooking, the water is likely to boil up and over. It is therefore a good idea to use either a vented lid or prop the lid open with a wooden cocktail stick, placing it between the lid and the rim of the dish. Use cling film if you prefer, making sure that it doesn't touch the vegetables directly and pull back one corner to vent. Another alternative is to use roasting bags, but since you cannot easily reposition the food in them, you will have to jiggle the bottom of the bag with an oven glove so that the centre pieces of vegetables are pushed towards the outside. If you are careful, the bags can be reused. Remember to loosely seal the roaster bags with a large elastic band and never use the metal tag. Allow about 6-8 minutes to cook a single portion and 10-14 minutes for four to five servings. You will be able to see how things are going when you test halfway through cooking. Cooking will continue if the vegetables are left in the boiling liquid and covered tightly.

Many people prefer to cook their vegetables earlier in the day and then reheat just before the meal. You must take this into consideration when cooking as the vegetables will cook a little further during the reheating process. Incidentally, when you reheat, remember to stir the vegetables during this time.

Among the vegetables that can be cooked whole are beetroot, swede, turnips and celeriac. These vegetables are very difficult to peel when they are raw but are so easy to peel once they are cooked. Try cooking them this way and you will never find yourself peeling your fingers rather than the vegetables again. Rinse off any earth clinging to the vegetables, then place large whole items singly in a bowl that is slightly larger in diameter than the vegetable itself. Several smaller vegetables, such as beetroots or turnips, can be cooked together in a larger bowl. Cut a thin slice from the base of large vegetables, but only snip off the longer stalk from beetroot. Put the vegetables in the bowl and add sufficient hot water to reach halfway up the sides – 285 ml/½ pint is usually sufficient. There is no need to add salt. Cover the bowl with a plate and cook on Full Power until you see the water boil (about 5 minutes). Using oven gloves, carefully remove the plate, turn the vegetables over and, if you are cooking several small vegetables together, reposition them so that the side that was towards the middle is now towards the outside. Re-cover and continue cooking for about 5-10 minutes. Test with a fork, then allow a few minutes standing time before testing again, because the vegetables are likely to soften further during this time. If after this time they are insufficiently cooked, add a little extra cooking time. Carefully remove from the bowl with a slotted spoon, place on a board and peel in a downwards direction using a knife and fork. Now you can slice or mash, adding seasoning and a little butter if you like.

Celeriac can be eaten as a cooked vegetable or as a salad ingredient and *céleri-rave* is a great favourite in France. It should, however, only be lightly cooked so that it can be grated. Allow only about 2 minutes after turning over when the water has boiled. Peel in the same way as the swede, although a sharper knife will be required, then grate coarsely and mix with French dressing and a little mayonnaise and season well with salt and pepper.

Beetroot should be cooked to the soft stage for serving sliced, or slightly under-cook for grating – when mixed with freshly chopped parsley and a little vinaigrette this makes a delightful salad.

Onions can be cooked whole, sliced or chopped, depending on what you want them for. Place the onions in a dish with only 2 or 3 tablespoons of water, then cover tightly and turn them over halfway through cooking. A large onion only takes about 5 minutes. Chopped onion does tend to stay crisp when used in casseroles, but if you cook the onion whole first and then chop it with the kitchen scissors, this will be avoided. Sweat onions in butter in a covered dish or sauté uncovered so that the steam can escape. Onions sauté and become tinged brown after about 5 minutes, but it is important to stir frequently to prevent parts of them becoming burnt.

Leeks, even for the experts, are difficult to cook so that they are not squeaky and yet are not soft and mushy. The secret is to cook them with a little butter or margarine added to the salted water. The fat has a tenderizing effect on this type of vegetable. Prepare leeks in the usual way, either sliced or whole, and add sufficient salted water to come halfway up the vegetable. Remember the knob of butter, then cover and cook, stirring once or twice during cooking – 450 g/1 lb of leeks takes about 6-7 minutes.

Vegetables with a high water content, such as marrow, courgettes and spinach, can be cooked without added water, but this rather depends upon the amount being cooked and the way that they are cut up.

Spinach should be washed thoroughly in several changes of cold water and the thick stalks removed. Pack the leaves into a large roasting bag with just the water that clings to the leaves after washing. Seal loosely with a large elastic band. Put the bag on a dish just in case there is a leak and try to arrange the bag so that the opening is at the top. Cook until the spinach packs down, then drain either into a colander or by grasping the bottom edges of the bag with an oven glove and allowing the water to drain through the opening. Season and chop if wished.

Courgettes should be topped and tailed but there is no need to peel them – they will cook best when cut up into batons. Sliced courgettes cook almost as well. Pile the courgettes into a shallow narrow dish and sprinkle with nutmeg. Cover tightly and cook until only just tender. Because they have a high water content, there will be quite a lot of residual heat which will soften the courgettes further. Carefully uncover, stir and season. You can cook whole courgettes in the microwave but if they are very large the tops will tend to dry out. Courgettes that are about 10 cm/4 inches long are attractive when cooked whole. Arrange them in a shallow dish and add about 2 tablespoons of water. Cover and cook for about 2 minutes, then reposition the courgettes, putting those in the middle towards the outside of the dish, re-cover and continue cooking for about 1 or 2 minutes.

Young marrows do not need to have their pulp and seeds removed, they cook very well and are very pleasant to eat. Top, tail and peel the marrow before slicing or cutting into chunks, then cook in 2 or 3 tablespoons of water to which you have added a teaspoon of oil or a knob of butter. Cover tightly and cook for about 3 minutes, then stir and reposition the pieces. Re-cover and continue cooking until just tender. A 1.8 kg/4 lb marrow will take about 10 minutes on Full Power.

Squash are a fairly new vegetable to the British market. They have much in common with marrows but I find them less watery. The skins are very tough. I have recently been experimenting with cooking squash and you might like to try using the same method as that used for cooking whole swede. A 450 g/1 lb green acorn squash will fit comfortably into a 1.5 litre/2½ pint bowl and cooks on Full Power in about 10 minutes. Remember to turn the vegetable over halfway through cooking. After cooking, cut in half, then remove the seeds before peeling and cutting up.

Runner beans, Brussels sprouts, shelled peas and **podded broad beans** can all be cooked in the same way as the sliced root vegetables. Add salted water to come halfway up the bowl. Cook them on Full Power, covered or vented, stirring or repositioning the vegetables once or twice during cooking. Allow between 7 and 12 minutes per 450 g/1 lb.

Mushrooms are better when cooked with 1 or 2 tablespoons of water and a little butter, but taste absolutely marvellous if you add a few drops of soy sauce and a dash of sherry. Mushrooms will only take 2 or 3 minutes to cook.

Cabbage requires only 3 or 4 tablespoons of salted water and a knob of butter to soften it, but if you are unable to stir or turn, you may find that the top of the cabbage starts to burn. Cabbage is difficult to cook on an automatic programme.

Tomatoes will collapse or burst if they are cooked whole. It is better to halve them and cook on the Defrost control and the more tomato halves that you cook at any one time, the less collapsing that will happen. Always take each tomato half out as soon as it is cooked. Tomatoes require no added water as they have a very high water content.

Corn-on-the-cob is fun to cook in the microwave. There is no need to remove the silk or the husk. Simply put the cobs in a dish or wrap in greaseproof paper or non-stick baking parchment and cook, turning occasionally, until they are cooked. Two cobs will probably only take about 7 minutes. If you are cooking several corn cobs at any one time, you will need to allow about 3 minutes per cob and these should be turned over and repositioned during cooking so that any that are in the centre are pushed towards the outside during the second half of the cooking time. Unwrap and test by lifting a corn kernel from the stem and, if it comes away reasonably easily, you know that the corn is sufficiently cooked.

Cauliflower and **broccoli** are more difficult to cook by microwave since the florets and the stems are such totally different textures. I find it is better to remove the thicker part of the stalk from broccoli and then slice it finely mixing it in with the florets for cooking. About 4 or 5 tablespoons of water is required and broccoli should be cooked and covered, stirring very frequently indeed – 450 g/1 lb of broccoli will take about 8 minutes. Similarly it is better to remove the florets from the cauliflower and cook in a little water. Cauliflower florets do cook quite quickly. Salt the water before stirring in the florets and cook covered, repositioning occasionally during cooking – 450 g/1 lb takes about 10 minutes. Cauliflower cooks much more during a standing time, so bear this in mind when cooking. If you do wish to cook a whole cauliflower, it is best to cook for longer but on the Defrost control, adding about 2.5 cm/1 inch of water to encourage the stem to cook and keeping the florets uppermost. Whole cauliflower is best cooked uncovered.

Aubergines do not need to be salted and drained before cooking in the microwave. Although a slight bitterness will remain, this will be masked when the aubergines are stuffed or sauced. Aubergines are a very good vegetable for combination cooking because they can be first cooked in the microwave and then be dipped in batter for deep-frying as fritters. To cook aubergines for stuffing, place the whole aubergine in a shallow dish, adding 5 or 6 tablespoons of water. Cover and cook until tender. Two medium aubergines will take about 7 minutes. You can then scoop out the pulp and complete the dish according to your usual recipe.

Globe artichokes are mainly a winter vegetable and there are seasonal fluctuations in price. Wash and trim in the usual way, removing the long stalk and place in a bowl with about 140-285 ml/¼-½ pint of water, depending upon how many artichokes you are cooking. Lightly salt the water and add a squeeze of lemon juice, then cover and cook on Full Power, turning the vegetables and repositioning once during cooking. The cooking times will depend upon how dry and how young the artichokes are, but on average 1 artichoke will take about 6 minutes and 4 artichokes about 16 minutes.

Asparagus is the most expensive of vegetables, so it would be a great disappointment to ruin this beautiful vegetable by overcooking. The smaller asparagus is wonderful when cooked by microwave. The thicker-stemmed asparagus must be peeled with a potato peeler and the thick end of the stem removed. You can find out how much to remove by bending the stem because the piece below the bend will be too tough to eat. Arrange the asparagus in two layers in a rectangular casserole so that half the stalks point in one direction and the other half in the opposite direction, and nestle the smaller spears towards the middle. Add about 140 ml/¼ pint of water, then cook, covered, on Full Power until the tips are just tender – 450 g/1 lb of asparagus takes about 9-14 minutes. Asparagus is lovely served with soured cream or Hollandaise sauce.

Jacket potatoes are quick to cook in the microwave. A medium-large potato takes about 4-5 minutes. If you are cooking more than 1 potato, you will be able to reduce the overall cooking time. Prick the potatoes well, place them in the microwave on kitchen paper and turn them over halfway through cooking. As soon as they are tender to the touch, wrap them in a clean cloth and leave for 10 minutes during which time they will complete cooking. If the potato is insufficiently cooked, you will find it very difficult to put things right. The only way to do this is the clamp the two halves together, wrap the potato and continue cooking. An easy way to make mashed potato is to cook large jacket potatoes in the microwave, then scoop out the pulp and mash with milk and butter and season with salt and pepper. Jacket potatoes are often a big selling point for the microwave oven because they take about an hour in the conventional oven compared to minutes in the microwave. Nevertheless, if you are going to cook, for example, 40 potatoes for a party, it would be cheaper and easier, and even more successful, to cook them all at once in the conventional oven. If you wish to have a crispy skin on microwave cooked potatoes, they can be popped under the grill.

Frozen vegetables Frozen vegetables require less water than fresh vegetables to cook and single portions need none at all. Always cook covered on Full Power. To deal with individual servings in sealed packages, slit the packet across the top and place on a plate. Most packets carry instructions for microwave cooking but about 2 minutes is usually sufficient for a 115 g/4 oz portion. Larger quantities require some water and 3 or 4 tablespoons is normally adequate. I cook these for about 5 minutes before testing. I rarely stir frozen vegetables during cooking, although you may prefer to do so.

Fish

Fish cooked by microwave is flavoursome and nutritious because it can be cooked without added liquid. You will notice after cooking fish this way that a certain amount of liquor comes from the fish. Do not throw this away – use it as the basis for a sauce. Fish takes about 4 minutes for 450 g/1 lb and it is mostly cooked on Full Power – the exception being large whole fish such as an entire salmon which, because it cannot be repositioned, would overcook at this speed. Cook fillets of fish covered either with a lid or suitable plastic film which is vented. Greaseproof paper tends to stick and non-stick baking parchment is inclined to be blown off by the cooling fan in the microwave. Arrange fish fillets in a single layer and tuck the tail end underneath to prevent this very thin part from overcooking. Should a large number of fillets be required, it is better to roll them up, although they can be cooked in two or three layers separated by pieces of non-stick baking parchment.

Bones, because they are hollow, attract microwaves and they get very hot. The flesh next to a bone is likely to pop and splatter, so you should always cover cutlets of fish during cooking. Do not uncover until the fish has had 1 minute standing time.

Fish fingers and fish cakes, because they are breaded, would soften too much if they were covered tightly but it is fine to cover them with kitchen paper. They will be crisper and nicer if they are cooked in a preheated browning dish to which 1 tablespoon of oil has been added. As soon as the dish is hot enough, press the fish fingers or fish cakes onto the hot surface and turn them over at once. They will need only 20-30 seconds additional cooking and should not be covered in the dish.

After gutting and cleaning, whole small fish, like herrings, trout or mackerel, should be slashed through the outer skin down the fin at the back. Otherwise, they are likely to splatter because the skin acts as a complete cover. Cook this type of fish *en papillote*, wrapping each fish separately in greaseproof or non-stick baking parchment. When the fish is cooked, it is a simple matter to remove the head and skin, taking out the bones if you wish and then these can be wrapped and thrown away in one easy stage. Large fish may have to be curved in order to fit on the turntable. Slash through the back in the same way as for small whole fish and shield the tail and head ends with smooth foil, overwrapping with greaseproof paper to make sure that the foil does not touch the sides of the oven, which would, of course, be dangerous and cause damage. The fish cannot be straightened out after cooking, but smaller fish will sometimes fit in diagonally in an oven without a turntable or in an oven where it is possible to reverse the turntable. There is very little microwave energy generated in the corners of the oven so overwrapping will not be necessary. Cook large fish on Defrost setting for about 8 minutes for 450 g/1 lb.

When using the browning dish for cooking cutlets, fillets or whole fish, first dip them in seasoned flour and you will find that browning will be more effective. Treat minced fish in the same way as fillets, arranging the fish balls in a circle around the edges of the dish and repositioning them once during cooking. White fish will naturally remain pale, but it is a simple matter to make a parsley or prawn sauce to serve as an accompaniment.

The microwave is very good for cooking fish with a strong aroma, such as smoked haddock, smoked cod and kippers. The cooking smells will be trapped inside the cavity. It is better to cover these fish fairly tightly with a lid and add 1 or 2 tablespoons of water to smoked haddock or cod if it is salty – which you can detect by smelling it. Smoked fish takes about the same length of time as fresh fish and is cooked on Full Power. An indication that kippers are cooked is when they begin to curve.

Poultry
All poultry will cook successfully by microwave and smaller birds will be better than larger. Roast poultry will not brown when cooked by microwave alone, but it may be

given added colour in other ways. A number of proprietary brands of microwave seasonings or paprika can be sprinkled on before cooking, or alternatively the chicken can be browned under the grill before serving. It is not particularly healthy to eat poultry skin as most of the fat lies just under the skin. Unless crispened, the skin tends to remain chewy. If you are going to carve the bird at the table and your diners are not microwave users themselves, they may find it somewhat unappetizing in appearance. Why not carve the bird in the kitchen before bringing it to the table; it can be made to look just as attractive if the legs and dark meat are skilfully arranged, perhaps alternating with the white breast meat.

Poultry must be completely defrosted before commencing cooking and this can be hastened using the microwave. To defrost, slit the underside of the plastic packaging and remove the metal tag. Put the chicken on a rack in a dish and heat on Full Power for about 2 minutes. At this stage the chicken will be too cold for cooking to accidentally commence. Reduce the setting to Defrost (35%) or a lower setting if you have one on your microwave and switch on for about 10 minutes. Remove the wrappings and throw away the juices. Continue microwaving, testing every 5 minutes, until the giblets can easily be pulled out. A 1.5 kg/3½ lb bird takes about 25 minutes. Put your hand inside the chicken and feel for ice crystals. If any remain, the chicken is not sufficiently thawed to be ready for cooking. Rinse in cold water until the crystals have completely disappeared.

There are several different ways of cooking chicken in the microwave. If you are particularly fussy, start with the chicken breast side down and then halfway through cooking reverse it. I personally do not bother to do this as, if I had to give the bird more attention than I would when cooking conventionally, I would feel it not worth while. Rub the breast with butter, sprinkle with paprika or microwave seasoning and place breast side up on a rack in a shallow dish. Tent with a slit roasting bag, tucking the edges of the bag into the dish. Cook on Full Power for 10 minutes regardless of size for any bird over 1.5 kg/3 lb. Reduce the setting to Defrost (35%) and continue cooking for about 25-40 minutes, depending upon the size and age of the chicken. The wing and leg tips will tend to burn unless they are shielded with foil. Wrap small pieces of foil around them halfway through the cooking period, but leave the roasting bag in position so that there is no chance of them touching the oven linings. There are various tests that can be carried out to ascertain whether the chicken is sufficiently cooked. One method is to use a meat thermometer, or the chicken can be cooked with a probe in position which should control the doneness. For me, the old-fashioned methods are always best. A good indication of doneness is when no pink juices show when the bird is slashed between the thigh and the body and the flesh is opaque as far as the bone. Another good way to test doneness is to twist the leg and the bone should then come away easily.

Turkeys up to 4.5 kg/10 lb can be cooked entirely by microwave. They must be completely thawed first and should be thawed on the Defrost or lower control in bursts of no more than 2 minutes per 450 g/1 lb. Each burst should be followed by 1 hour's rest. Turn the turkey over after each defrosting period and then finish with a rinse in cold water. Cook on a dish in the same way as for chicken, basting away the fat as it occurs, and start off by allowing 2 minutes per 450 g/1 lb on Full Power, followed by 12-15 minutes per 450 g/1 lb on the Defrost setting.

Chicken casseroles are easy to cook by microwave and take about 30 minutes. If a brown appearance is desired, the pieces will have to be browned in the browning dish, in a frying pan or under the grill first. No special rules need be applied, save for the necessity to turn the pieces over and reposition them once during cooking and, of course, to cook in a covered casserole. So many recipes call for cooked chicken and the colour of the skin will not be important in these cases. A 1.5 kg/3 lb chicken yields only about 350 g/12 oz of flesh so you may find it more economical to buy skinned chicken pieces, boned breasts or thighs. When the family prefers plain cooking, or a person dining alone requires a quick chicken meal, there can be no tastier dish than a crumbed, micro-fried chicken breast. To prepare this, all you have to do is to cut out any white sinews because these would splatter in the microwave. Dip in egg and golden crumbs or crushed cornflakes (there are now on the market coloured crumbs without all those additives). Put 1 or 2 tablespoons of oil in a shallow dish and, without covering, heat on Full Power for 2 minutes. Place the crumbed chicken breast side down in the oil, cover with greaseproof paper and cook for 1 minute. Wait for 30 seconds, then turn the chicken over and cook for a further minute. Drain the chicken piece on kitchen paper before serving. Up to 4 or 6 chicken breasts can be cooked this way, provided they are repositioned when turning them over. Only 2 minutes are required to heat the oil, although you will have to allow approximately 1½ minutes for each chicken breast.

There is nothing to beat home-made chicken stock. Put all the bits of skin, bone and carcass in the largest bowl that you can find. A 2.8 litre/5 pint bowl is usually about the right size. Add a piece of carrot, a piece of onion and a few herbs if you like and just cover with water. Three-quarters cover the top of the bowl with cling film and cook on Full Power for 35-45 minutes. Strain, then, when cool, refrigerate or freeze to allow the fat to set on the top. Remove the fat and you will find that you have a very good stock indeed. There is no need to confine stock-making to large quantities and, if you wish to be really economical, you can use the bone and skin from a chicken piece to make 150 ml/¼ pint of stock for use as a sauce next time. Naturally you will need less liquid and a smaller bowl, but the cooking time will only be reduced by about 10 minutes.

Meat
Any minced raw meat will cook quickly and thoroughly in the microwave. Minced meat balls only take about 5 minutes per 450 g/1 lb and a meat loaf will take about 10 minutes. Both can be cooked on Full Power. Meat loaves are satisfactory cooked in a loaf-shaped dish, but are even better if you cook them in a ring mould. Minced beef will brown after a short standing time even though the browning is not of the same glossy kind as when baked or fried. This applies equally to burgers. A single burger will only take about 1 minute cooked from frozen. You can always start off mincemeat

balls or burgers in the browning dish if you want to. The reason that mince is so good in the microwave is because it has been tenderized as the pieces of meat and gristle are ground down. Tough cuts of meat will not tenderize in the microwave, so if you are adamant about cooking casseroles, particularly casseroled beef, by microwave it is a good idea to tenderize it while it is raw. Meat tenderizer, which comes from the paw-paw, has a remarkable effect after only 30 minutes when sprinkled over meat. Other methods of tenderizing are beating with a cleaver or marinating. When the meat is cut into small cubes and cooked in a large quantity of liquid and set on the Defrost control, a more tender result will be attained, but you may find that the saving in time is not as much as you might have hoped. Veal, lamb and pork casseroles are successful because the meat starts off by being more tender. Casseroled beef cooked by microwave will be flavoursome, but the texture will be about the same as a fillet or rump steak – in other words, it has to be chewed rather than melts in the mouth.

I only recommend cooking steaks in the microwave if they are cooked in the browning dish. Preheat the browning dish, add a knob of butter, then seal the steak on both sides before continuing to cook. About 1 minute per steak is usually sufficient. Chops in casseroles are perfectly satisfactory, but once again, unless the browning dish is used, the meat will look pale or grey.

Roasts are very good in a microwave if an even shape is chosen. A flatter, wider joint will cook more successfully than a rolled narrow joint, since microwaves cook to a depth of 2.5 cm/1 inch all around the outside and the middle is cooked by conduction. After roasting, tent joints with foil and leave to stand for 10-15 minutes before carving. Roast joints on a rack in a shallow dish; the larger the joint, the more browning will be achieved but the less even will be the cooking.

Roast lamb, roast pork and roast bacon joints are highly successful and can be cooked in the same way as roast beef. Bacon joints should not be too crisp and therefore should be cooked covered. Unless very large, roasts can be cooked on Full Power, although cooking will be more even if they are cooked on half power (50%). As a guide, allow 6-9 minutes per 450 g/1 lb for beef, depending upon how rare you like it; 8-10 minutes for lamb; 8½-9 minutes for veal. It is essential to cook pork fully (9-10 minutes per 450 g/1 lb on Full Power). Allow between 11 and 17 minutes per 450 g/1 lb for any roast meat cooked on medium. If you are using a microwave thermometer, you may like to know that it should read 70-75°C/160-170°F for a well-cooked joint. At the end of the cooking time, after the joint has stood tented for 10-15 minutes, the temperature will rise by 10°C/20°F. You may find when you use a meat thermometer to test that you will get very different readings in different parts of the joint. This should equal out after the recommended standing time, but you can always give added time if it is necessary.

Sausages

When cooked in the microwave, sausages will remain pale and no amount of cooking will improve matters. If they are overcooked in the microwave, they become spongy and hard inside. To obtain some sort of colouring, a browning dish is a must, and browning will be deeper if the sausages are slightly warmed before cooking them this way. Put the separated sausages on a plate or paper in the microwave and heat on Defrost (35%) for about 30 seconds. Leave the sausages to stand while heating the browning dish to maximum, then add a dab of butter and the sausages, flipping them over so that they brown on all sides. Only a further minute or two will be required. Cook the sausages, without covering, on Full Power. Four sausages will take about 4 minutes, depending upon how fatty the sausagemeat is. Sausages can be thawed in the microwave on the Defrost setting, allowing about 1 minute per sausage. To cook sausages for a family, it is much better to par cook in the microwave and then complete browning under the grill or in a frying pan. Frankfurters are ready cooked and therefore only need re-heating – 15-20 seconds on Full Power should be sufficient time for each frankfurter.

Bacon rashers To cook a couple of bacon rashers quickly, place them side-by-side on a piece of kitchen paper and cover with another piece of kitchen paper, making sure that the pattern side is not against the bacon. Cook on Full Power, allowing 30 seconds for 1 rasher or 45 seconds for 2 rashers. Remove the bacon rashers from the paper immediately to prevent them from sticking. To cook several rashers of bacon, it is better to overlap them on a plate or dish, then cover them with kitchen paper. Allow a similar cooking time, then remove the paper and either mop up the fat on the plate or transfer the rashers to a clean, warm plate. Crispy, brown bacon must be cooked in a preheated browning dish. Preheat the empty dish on Full Power for about 2 minutes, then add the bacon rashers and, without covering, cook for about 30 seconds. Immediately turn the bacon rashers over, repositioning them if possible, then continue cooking for about 20 seconds for 4 rashers.

Fruit

Microwaving is the very best method for stewing fruit whether it is fresh or dried. As with cooking in a casserole in the conventional oven, the fruit can be cooked covered to prevent too much evaporation, and therefore requires little or no added liquid. It is very difficult to stew fruit in a pan on the hob unless the heat is very low or a considerable amount of liquid is used, because the fruit is likely to burn on the bottom of the saucepan. Always prick fruit such as gooseberries before cooking, otherwise they tend to explode (although this is not very serious). Cover dried fruit with a generous amount of water and cook covered but vented. If the fruit protrudes above the water level, these parts will dry up. Stirring is a good idea during cooking. Three or four servings of stewed prunes or apricots should only take about 7 minutes. Stewed fresh fruit will take about the same length of time.

Cakes and Puddings

An average-sized large cake takes about 4-6 minutes to cook on Full Power and 6 small cakes take about 1¼ minutes on Full Power. A two-layered cake such as a Victoria sandwich will take about 2 minutes for each half. If your oven has a shelf, it is possible to cook these simultaneously, allowing a little more time. Otherwise, cook them separately. Some cakes are truly wonderful when cooked by microwave and others will turn out as dry as wood. This will depend upon the recipe used. It is the choice of ingredients that counts, and cakes containing cocoa or melted chocolate or those made by the melting method using golden syrup are definitely more moist. Cakes will not brown in the microwave and, if pale ingredients are used, a pale cake will be the result. The microwave oven has no dry heat to brown and crispen the outer surface. Obviously, chocolate cakes will appear more attractive and rich fruit cakes will also be fairly appetizing to look at.

Microwaved cakes stale quickly because they do not have a protecting crust. The moisture within them quickly evaporates and they become hard on the outside. To overcome this, wrap microwaved cakes in cling film or foil immediately upon cooling. Another way to keep microwaved cakes fresh is to ice them and this will form a wrapping and also give colour to an otherwise unacceptably pale finish. Choose the bakeware carefully: round shapes should be no more than 18 cm/7 inches in diameter, and loaf shapes are better when they are only twice as long as wide. Cakes cook very well in ring moulds, as the centre of the cake is the last to cook and, if there is no centre there is no problem. Small cakes can either be cooked in double paper cases, popping one inside the other, or in specialist bun pans.

Cakes cooked in a microwave rise considerably during cooking and are ready when they are just dry on top. Immediately they are cooked, the mixture will drop back. This is quite normal and does not affect the cake, except that all microwaved cakes have a slightly more dense texture. The cake mixture will double in height during cooking, but as there is no dry heat to set the mixture on top, any mixture that rises above the level of the dish will simply run out over the sides. It is essential, therefore, to have a dish large enough to contain the fully-cooked cake.

There is quite a build up of moisture in the base of the cake dish and sometimes this can cause sticking, making it difficult to turn the cake out. Except when using plastic bakeware, grease and base line with a circle of non-stick baking parchment. There is a considerable amount of carry-over cooking because of the moisture trapped in the base, so that cakes should be left for a full 5 minutes before turning out and during this time any undercooked mixture underneath will catch up. When cooking cakes by microwave, add a little extra liquid, since more moisture is evaporated off during cooking.

As a rule, cook cakes uncovered on Full Power, the exception being fruit cakes which benefit from the longer cooking to develop the colour which is attainable when cooked on the Defrost setting.

There are so many different kinds of puddings that you can make using the microwave that it would be really quite impossible to describe them all in just a few words. All sponge puddings that would normally be steamed cook well in the microwave and you can use any conventional recipe for this. I would suggest that light brown sugar is substituted for white sugar so that the pudding has added colour. All the rules that apply to cakes apply to these puddings, except that if you are making a jam or syrup pudding with the syrup in the base, you must choose a dish that is totally heatproof, otherwise it could scar or develop holes due to the very high temperature that the syrup or jam would reach. Although microwaved sponge puddings do not brown, they are extremely attractive because of the syrup or jam toppings. A rather nice idea is to melt about 115 g/4 oz of chocolate, then pour it over the pudding and serve it either hot immediately or cold later.

Other kinds of pudding that are good in a microwave include crumbles; these need to be cooked in a deep dish because of the chances of the fruit boiling up. In nearly every case, the fruit will boil up the sides and slightly spill onto the top of the crumble, but this enhances the appearance rather than detracting from it.

If you wish to make fruit puddings such as crumbles by microwave, add the crumble topping in the usual way. Cook by microwave until the topping is firm but not hard and then, if you wish, brown under the grill. Sometimes a sprinkling of demerara sugar added before microwaving gives a good finished appearance as the sugar does not dissolve. So many fruit desserts require cooked fruit that it is possible to aid the cooking of fools and pies by first cooking the fruit in the microwave.

Egg custards, bread and butter puddings, etc., and all those puddings that rely upon a thickening of eggs with milk, should be cooked on the Defrost control and this will take about 12 minutes. If you heat the milk before beating in the eggs, the pudding will cook more evenly. Crème caramel is a popular dessert that many people refrain from cooking simply because of the difficulties of making the syrup. Syrups are one of the processes at which the microwave excels, whether it be a simple syrup to serve with fruit salad, the deeper syrup to serve with caramel oranges, or a dark syrup to pour over nuts to make nut brittle. There is always a danger when making syrups that they will overcook and blacken and burn and this can happen whether they are cooked in a saucepan or in a heatproof jug in the microwave. Always remove the jug carefully, making sure that you hold the handle only as the jug will become too hot to hold, and do this before the syrup darkens to the required colour. During standing time, the syrup continues cooking, so that if it were to be taken out of the microwave when brown, it would certainly be black by the time it was poured out.

Jams and Chutneys

Compare a microwaved jam with one that you have bought in the shops and you will be amazed at the difference between them. Most commercial jams have added pectin but this is not necessary when cooking small quantities by microwave. There is no flavour other than that of the fruit and this is why microwaved jams are so superior. The best flavour and colour will be achieved when only small quantities are cooked, since the longer jams have to be boiled, the darker and more bitter they become. The rules for jam making are first of all to use a bowl that is really heatproof, such as a pyrex bowl (plastic bowls are unsuitable unless the manufacturers' recommend them). Cook in small quantities and never more than 450 g/1 lb of fruit at a time (although up to 2.25 kg/5 lb can be made in the 2.8 litre/5 pint bowl).

The soft berries, such as blackberries, raspberries, strawberries and loganberries, are by far the easiest to cook. Add 225 g/8 oz of sugar to each 225 g/8 oz of berries – it doesn't matter whether the berries are fresh or frozen. Stir until all the sugar is moist and coloured. Without covering, heat on Full Power (about 4 minutes). Stir the mixture gently until all the sugar has dissolved, then cook uncovered on Full Power without stirring until there is a slight wrinkling of the syrup when a little is poured onto a cold plate and pushed with the back of a spoon (about 7 minutes). Do not expect a very firm set as the jam sets quite firmly upon cooling.

Blackcurrants, redcurrants, gooseberries and fruit with tougher, smooth skins must be cooked in a little water before the sugar is added. If this is not done, the skins will become very tough. Put the fruit in a large bowl with a few tablespoons of water, three-quarters cover and cook, stirring occasionally, until the fruit softens (about 7 minutes). Uncover and stir in the sugar until it has dissolved – this will take place quickly since the fruit is hot. Without further covering, cook until setting point is reached (about 12 minutes, depending upon the quantity). Plum and damson jam require no additional water and a little less cooking than the tougher-skinned berries. Use the same proportions of sugar to fruit and you can use up to 900 g/2 lb of each. Cooking will take approximately half as long again.

To make marmalade, cook the whole fruit in a very large bowl in 285 ml/½ pint of boiling water. Cover with a plate and cook on Full Power for 20-25 minutes, turning the fruit over halfway through cooking. At the end of this time, the fruit is soft and may start to collapse, and this is an indication that it is ready. Carefully remove the plate using oven gloves, then take out the fruit, cut it into quarters and remove the pips. Shred the peel finely, discarding some of the pith. Return the shredded peel to the liquid in the bowl and stir in 675 g/1½ lb sugar. Without covering, cook on Full Power until the mixture is hot (about 3 minutes). Stir until the sugar has dissolved, then continue cooking until setting point is reached (about 12-20 minutes).

Chutneys need a long cooking time in order to thicken and darken. When cooked conventionally, there is a very real danger that the mixture will burn on the bottom, since it contains a large amount of sugar, so frequent stirring is advisable. In the microwave this burning cannot occur, but occasional stirring is still required as thick chutney tends to bubble and splatter. About 1.5 kg/3 lb of chutney will take approximately 35 minutes when cooked on Full Power. Most conventional recipes can be adapted.

Beverages
Use the microwave to heat up to four mugs of liquid to make tea, coffee, cocoa or chocolate, but do not overfill the mugs, particularly when heating milk as it tends to boil over. Stir liquids gently with a fork before heating to remove any air bubbles which will cause splattering – 140 ml/¼ pint of water will take about 1¾ minutes to reach boiling point; 285 ml/½ pint of water will take about 3¼ minutes; and 600 ml/1 pint of water will take about 6 minutes. A cup of coffee takes about 1¾ minutes to heat. When dealing with milk, allow about 1½ minutes for 140 ml/¼ pint, 2½ minutes for 285 ml/½ pint, and about 4 minutes to bring 570 ml/1 pint of milk to boiling point. Always stir liquids thoroughly before serving.

INDEX

Page numbers in italics refer to recipes illustrated